Intro

My last book came out 5 YEARS ago, and, uh... a lot's happened since then, huh?

A lot of us changed. We all took time to gaze inward and take a good hard look at the people we thought we were. Some of us acknowledged that maybe there's a little more to it than what we already have going on. In my case - a fox appeared!(We'll get deeper into that later.)

I'm sure a lot of you have been going through it and to be honest, me too!

Many events have taken place to really change things in mine and everyone's lives, but one thing that's remained consistent is my desire to draw, and draw for folks in this lovely fandom of ours.

So I hope that you enjoy some of the highlights of the last 5 years.I'm very happy to see that as I approach my 40th year on this planet, that I'm still growing and improving.

Additionally making some straight up kinky as F#$% art.

-Donryu

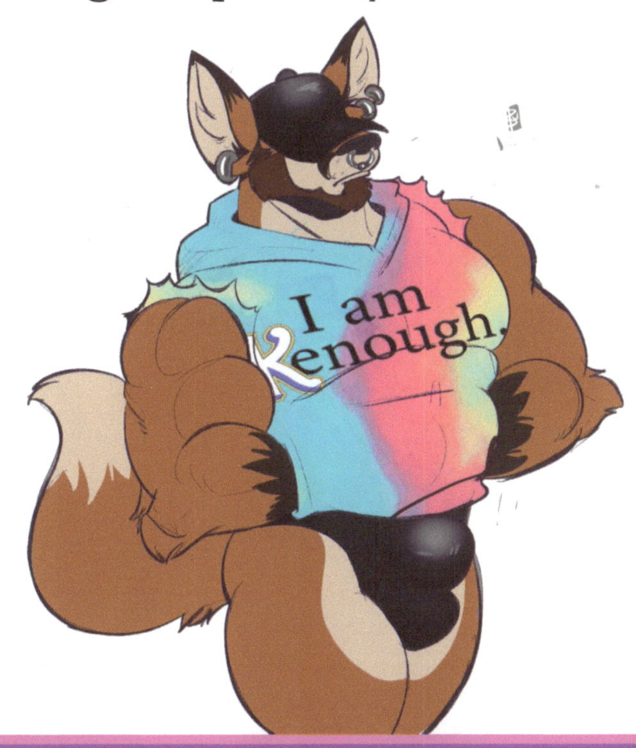

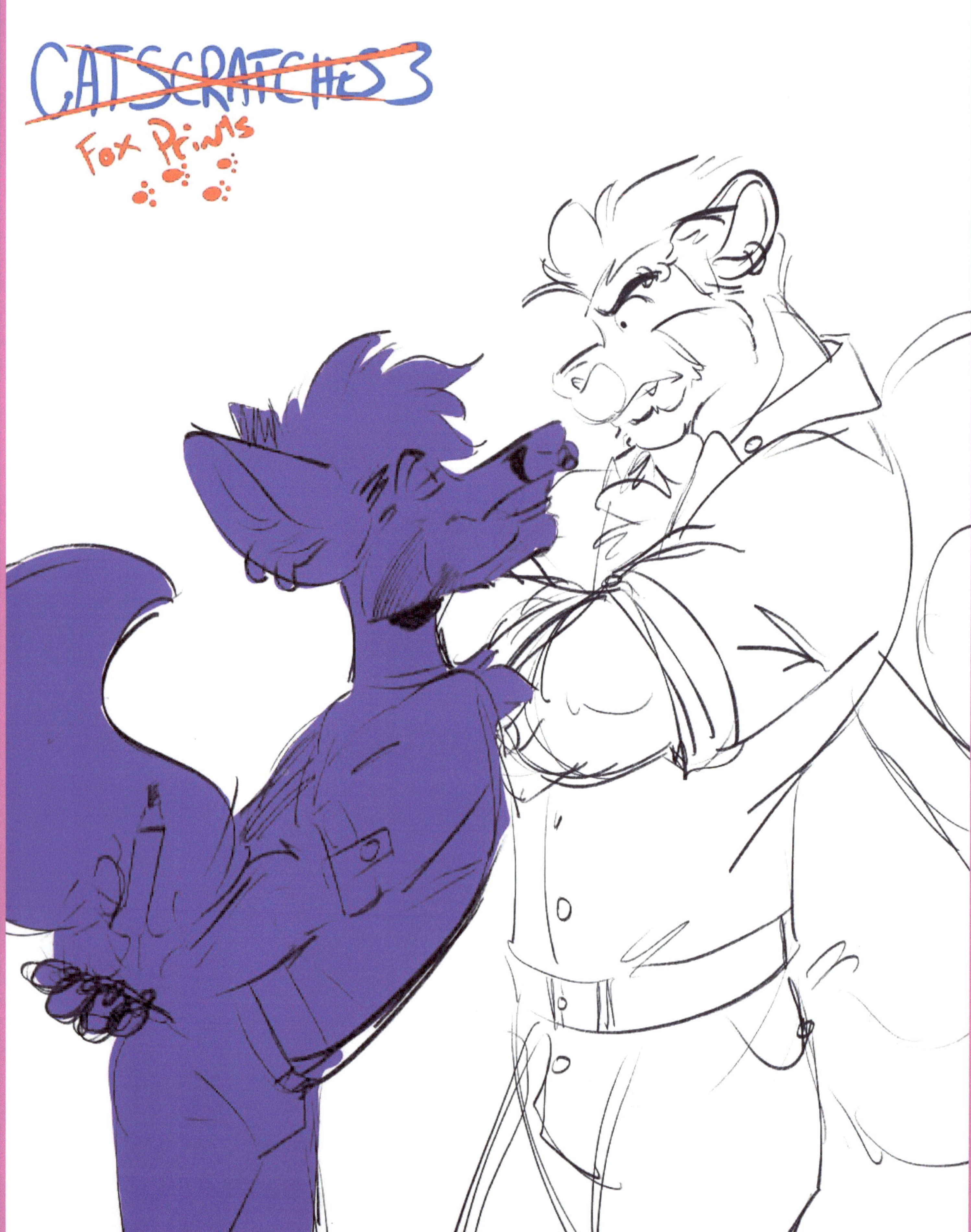
CATSCRATCHES 3
Fox Prints

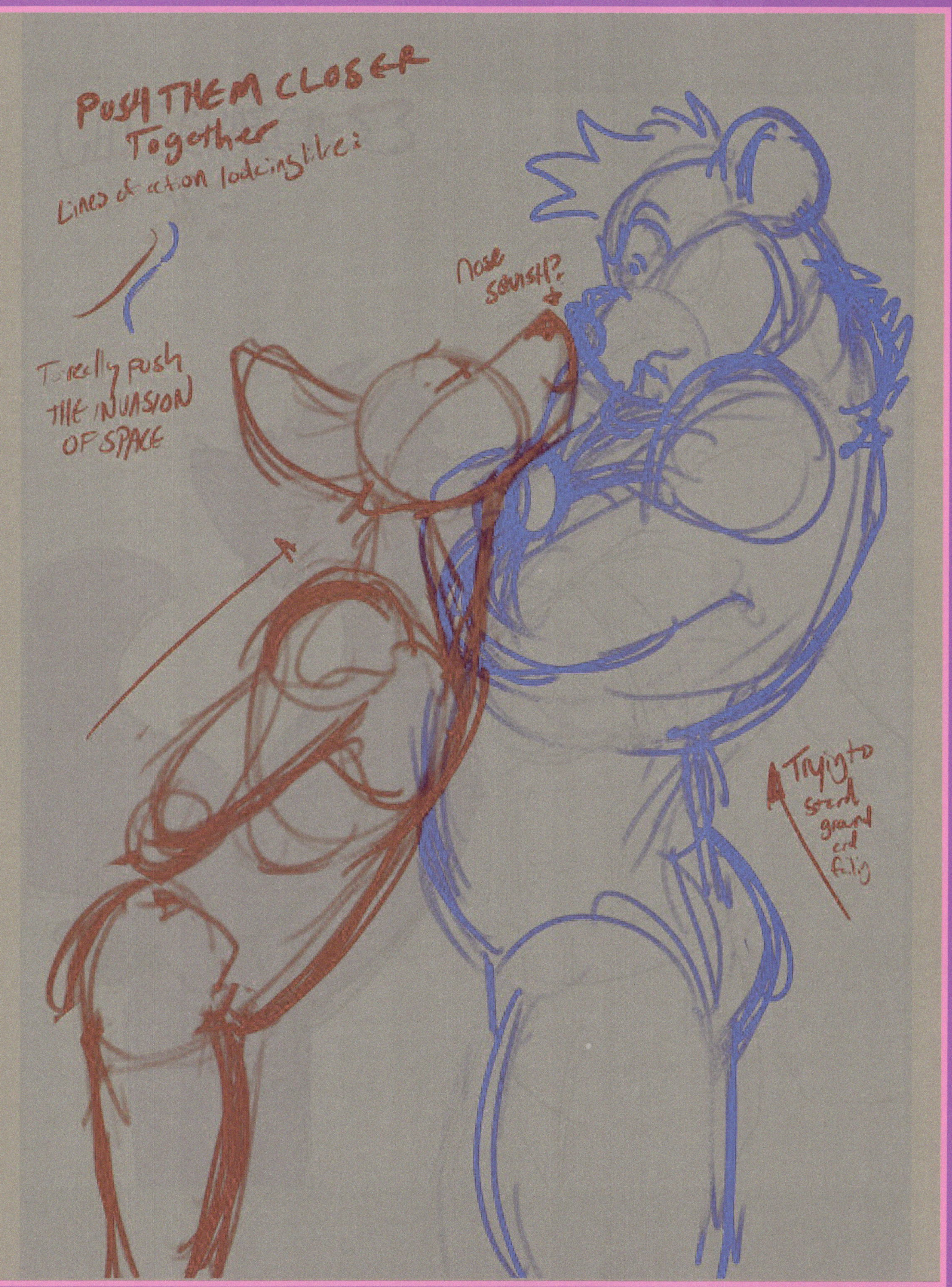

PUSH THEM CLOSER
Together
Lines of action looking like:
To really push
THE INVASION
OF SPACE
Nose
squish?
Trying to

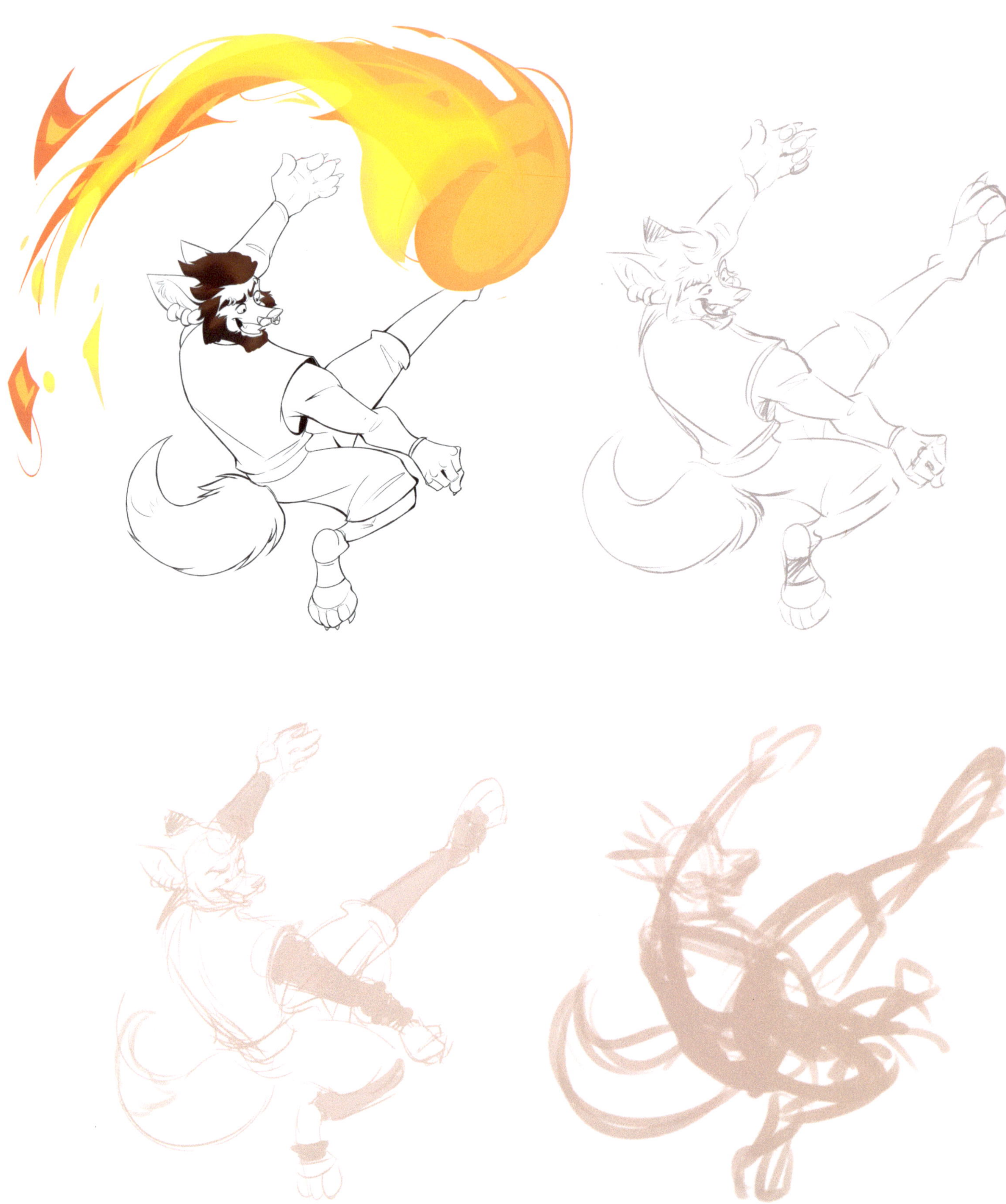

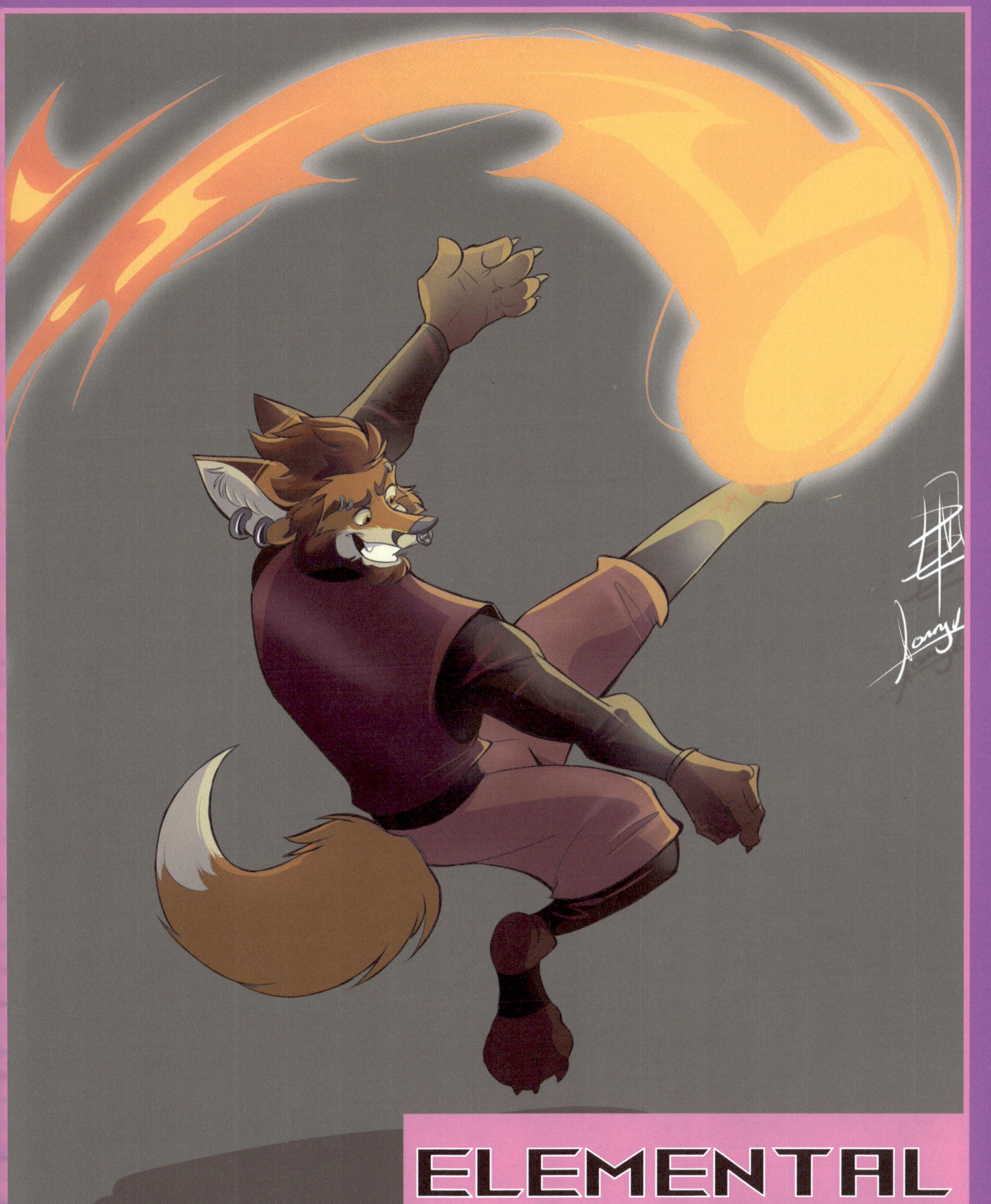

ELEMENTAL ARTS

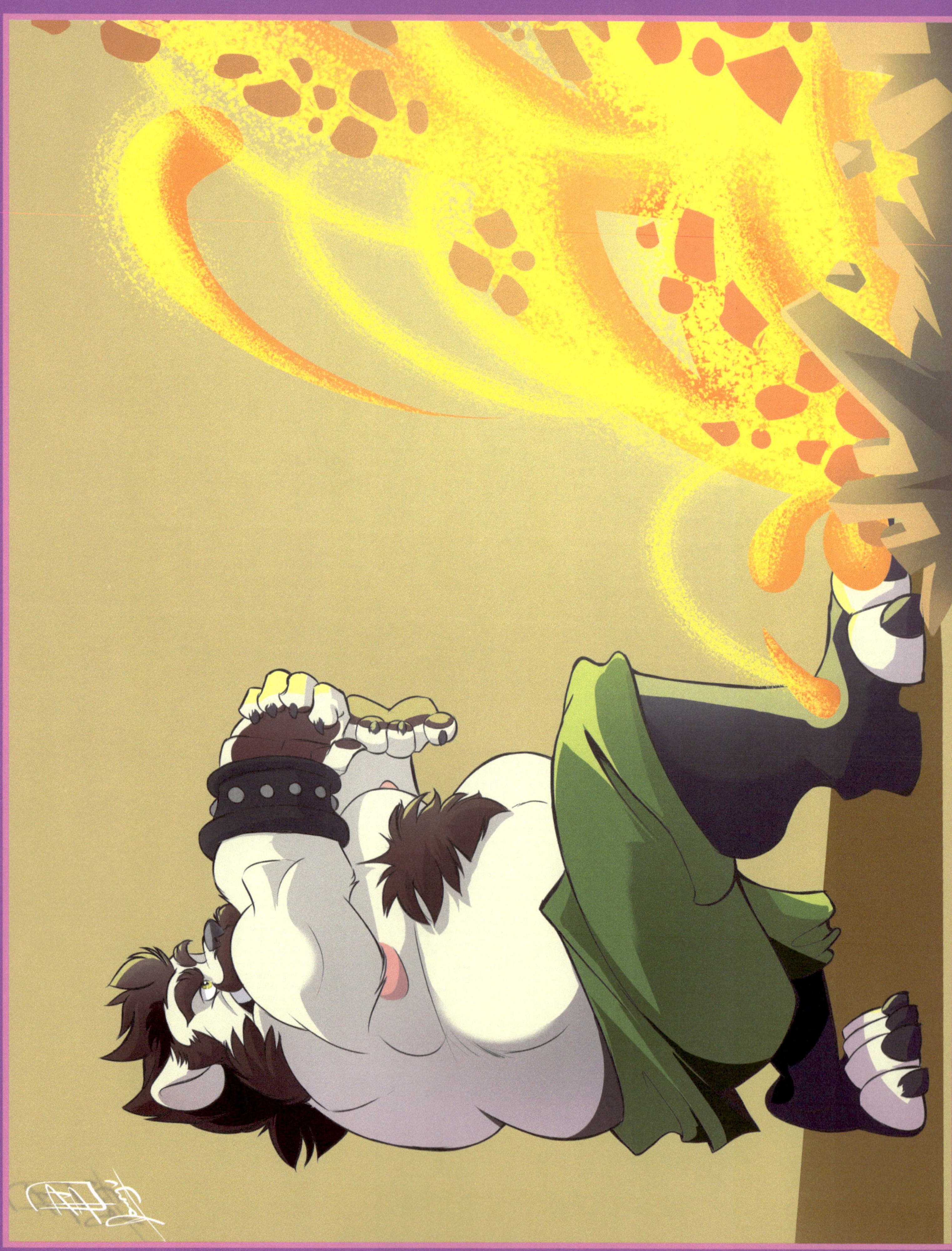

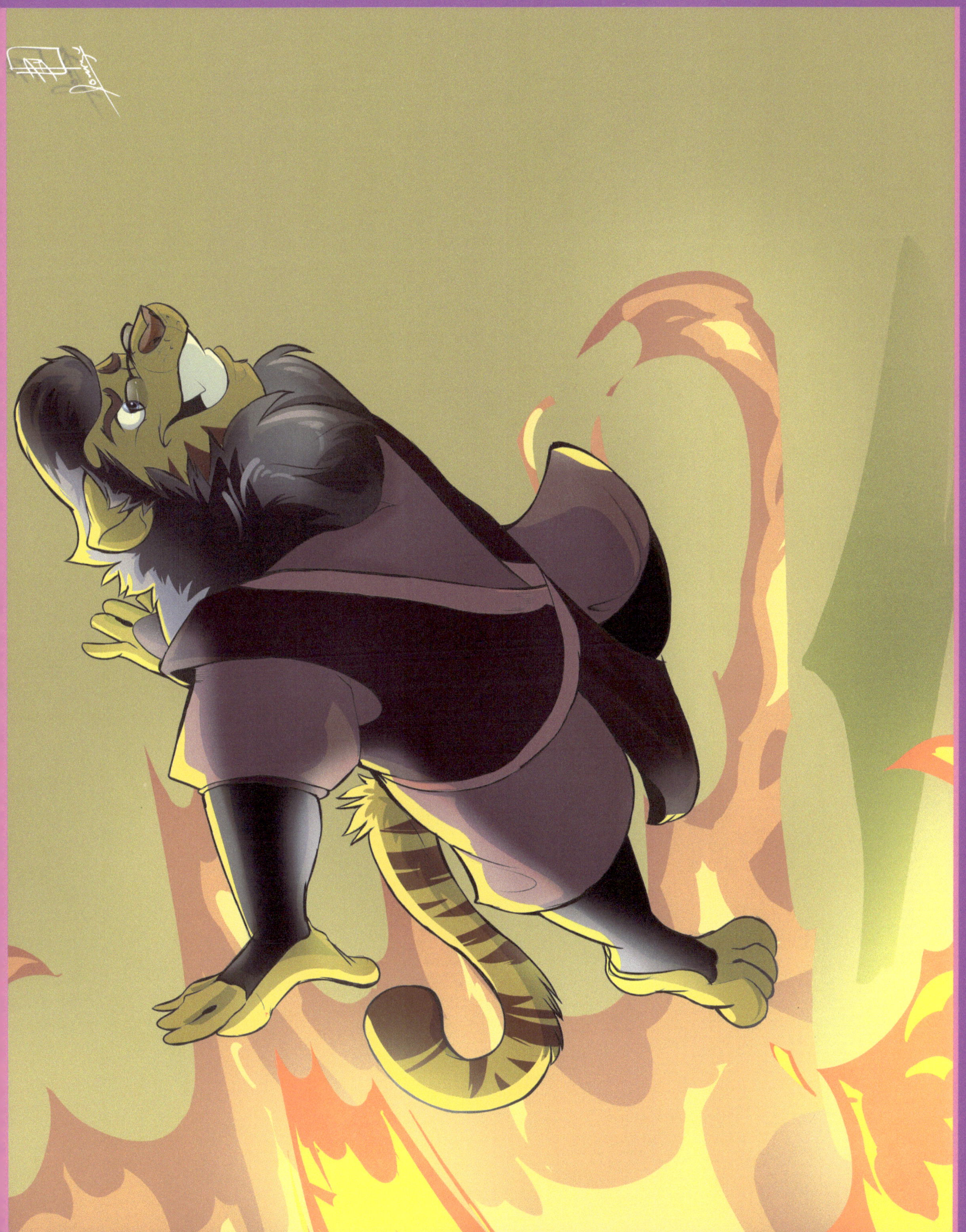

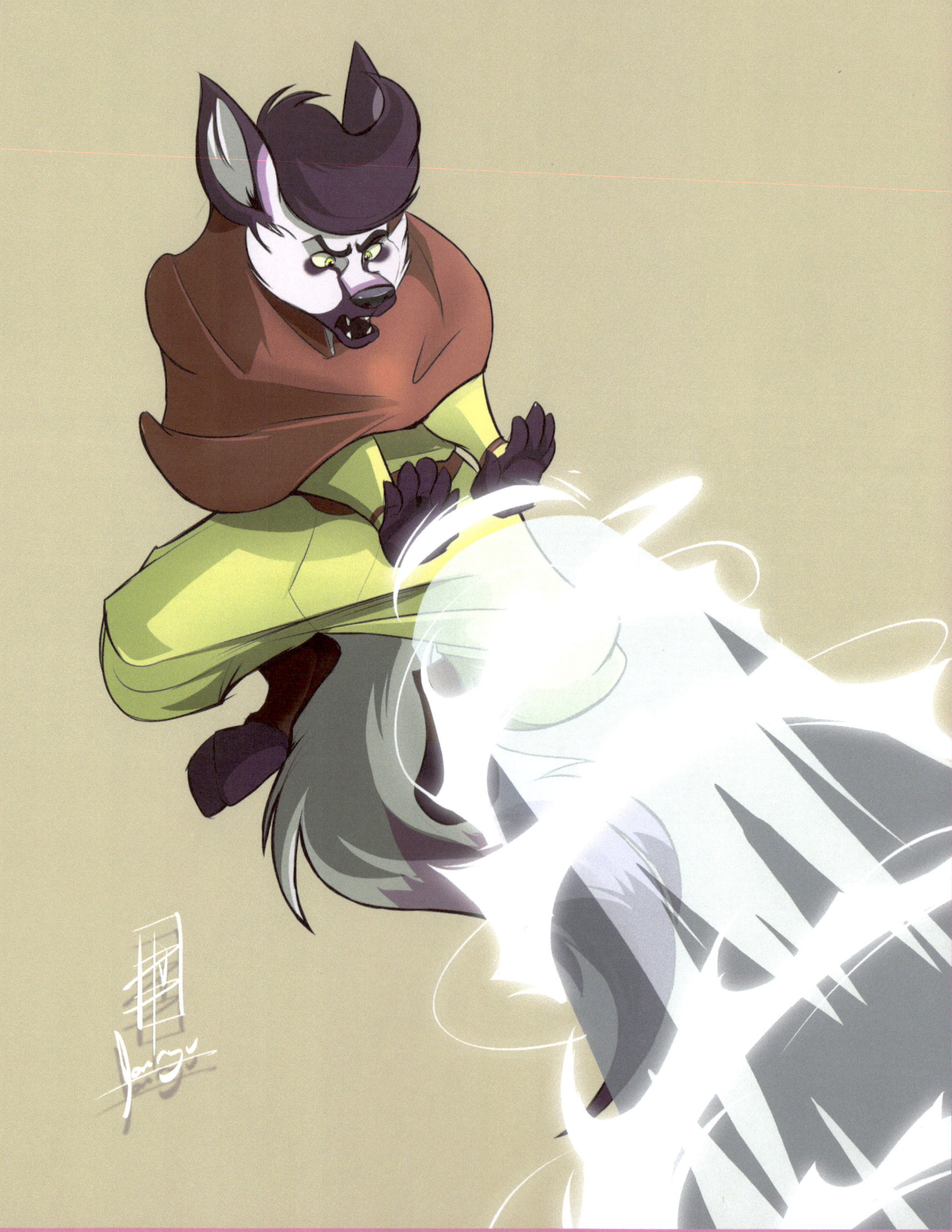

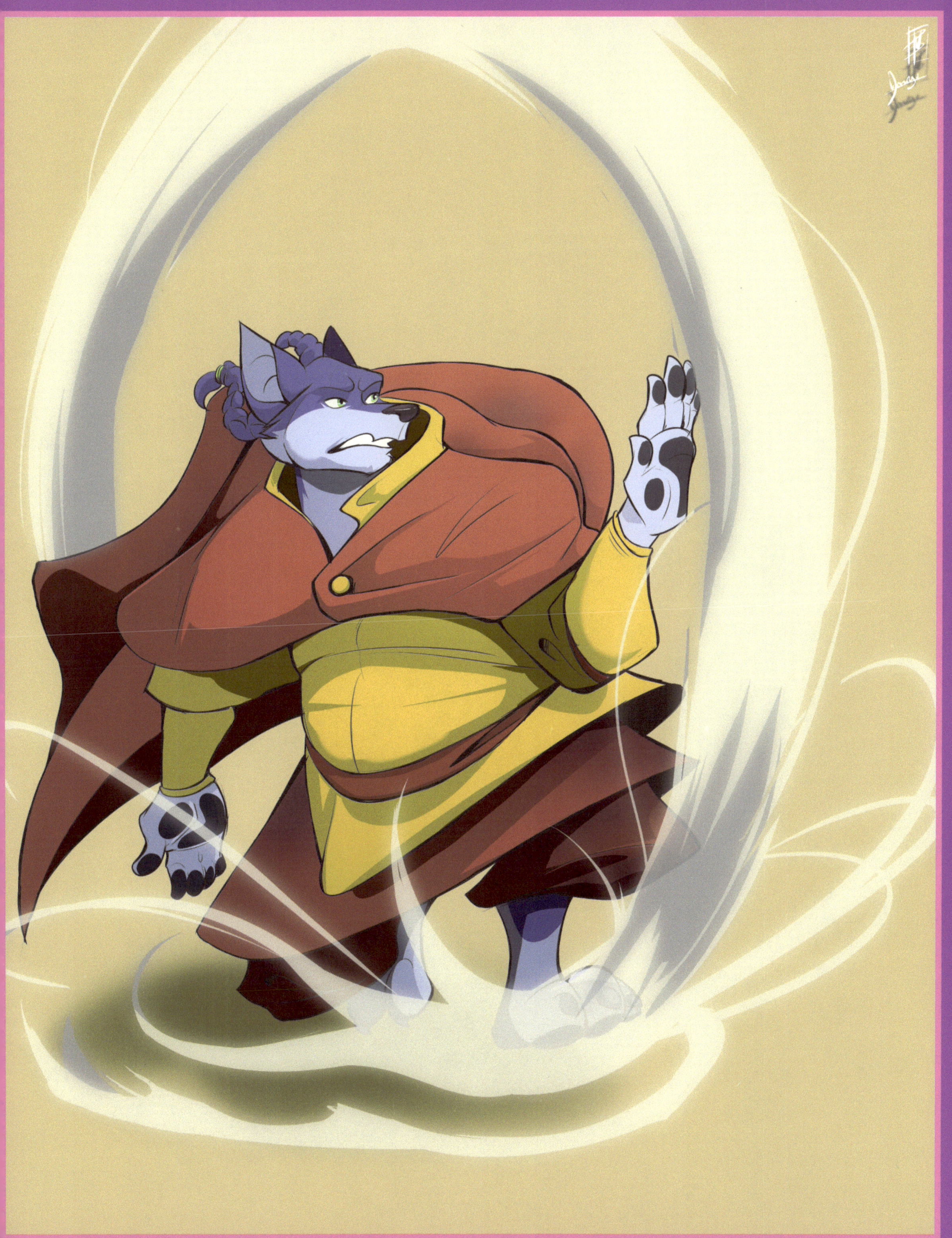

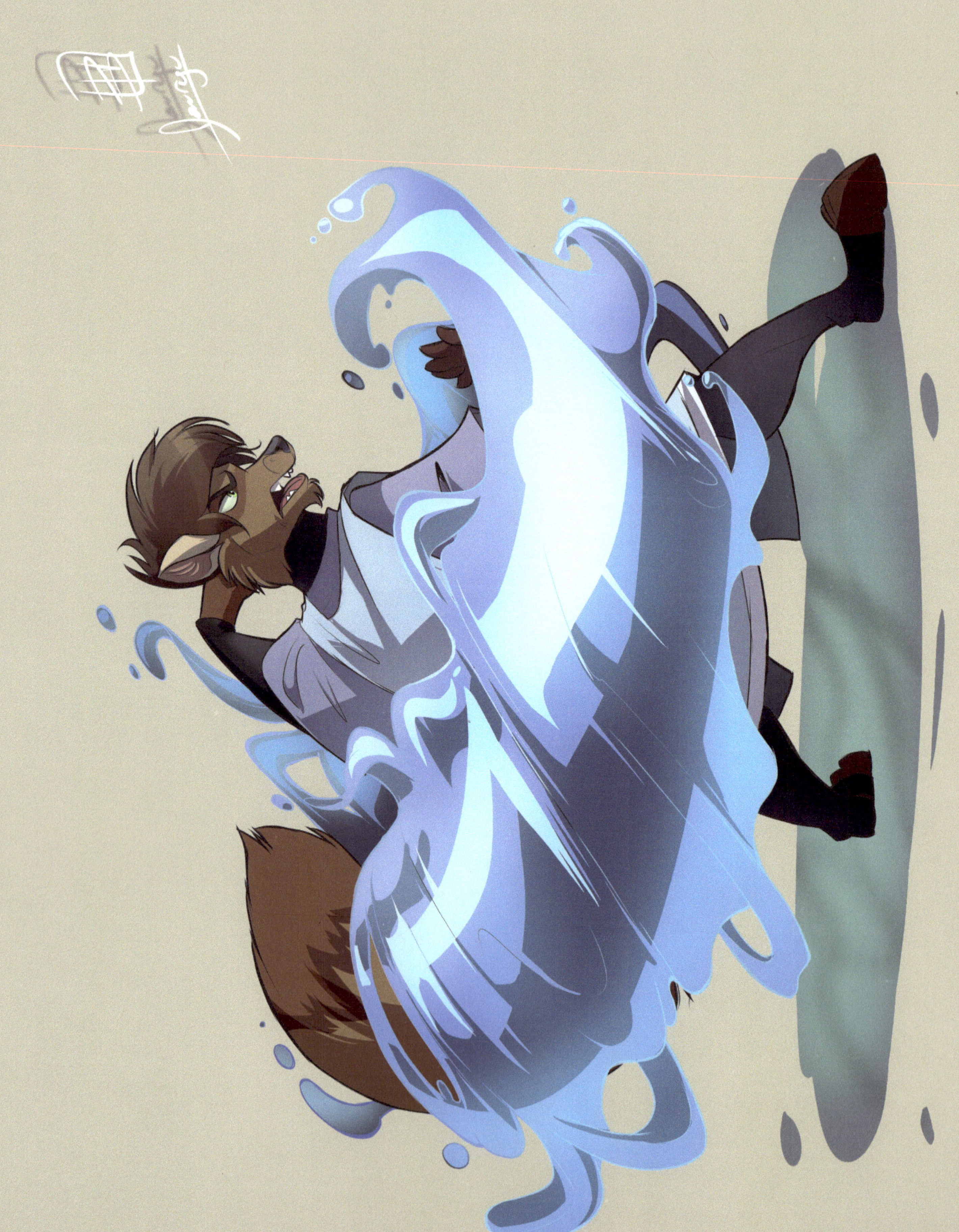

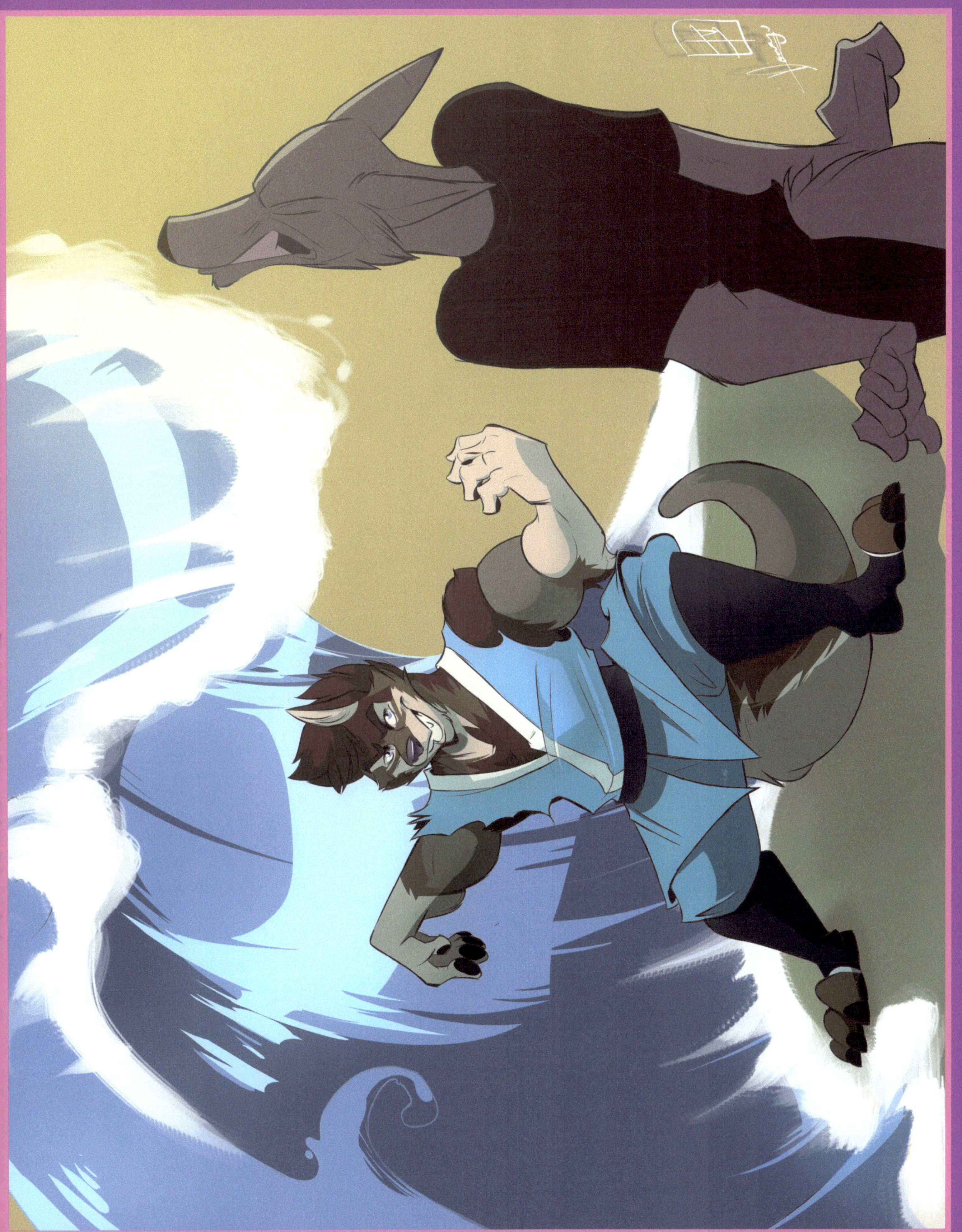

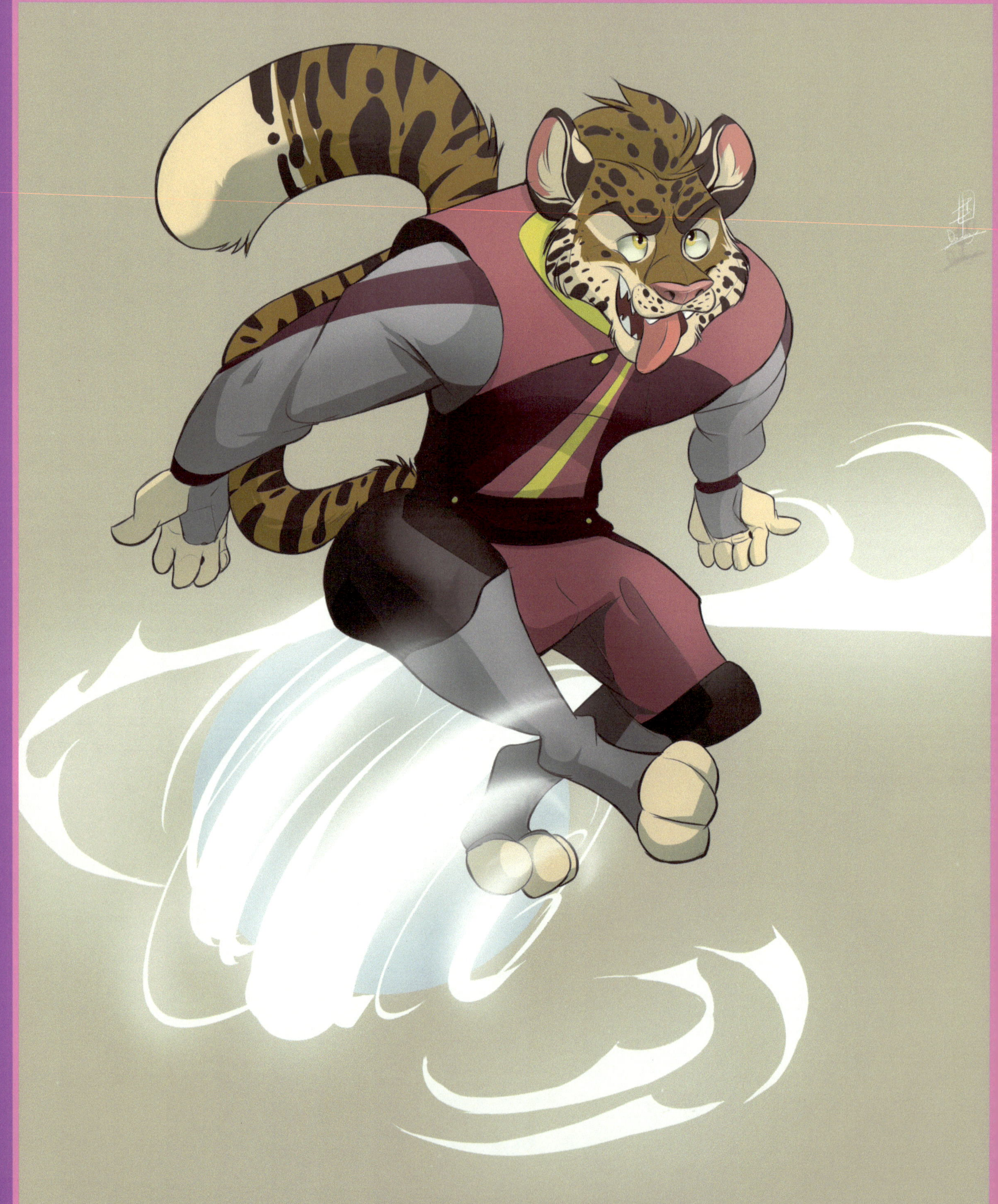

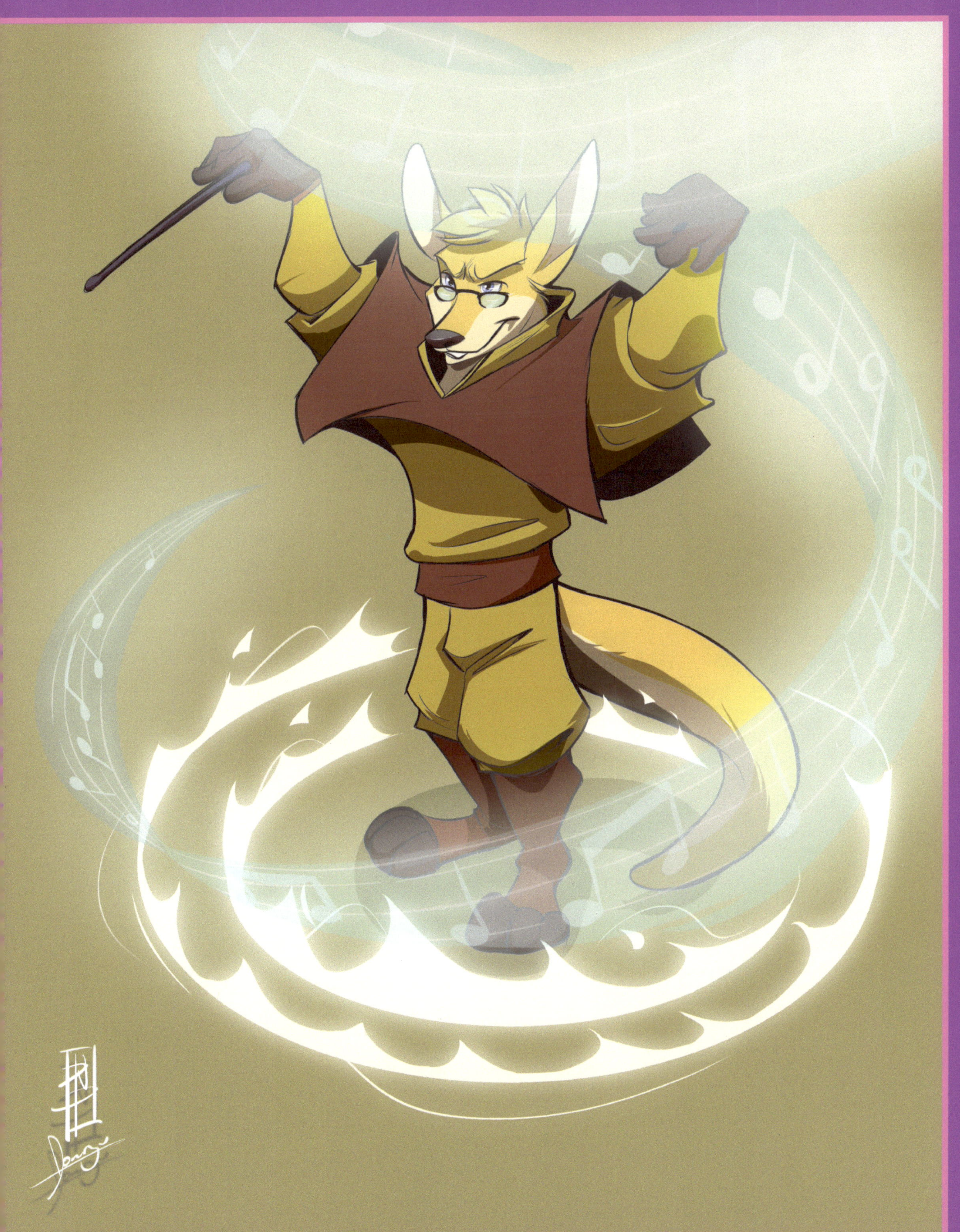

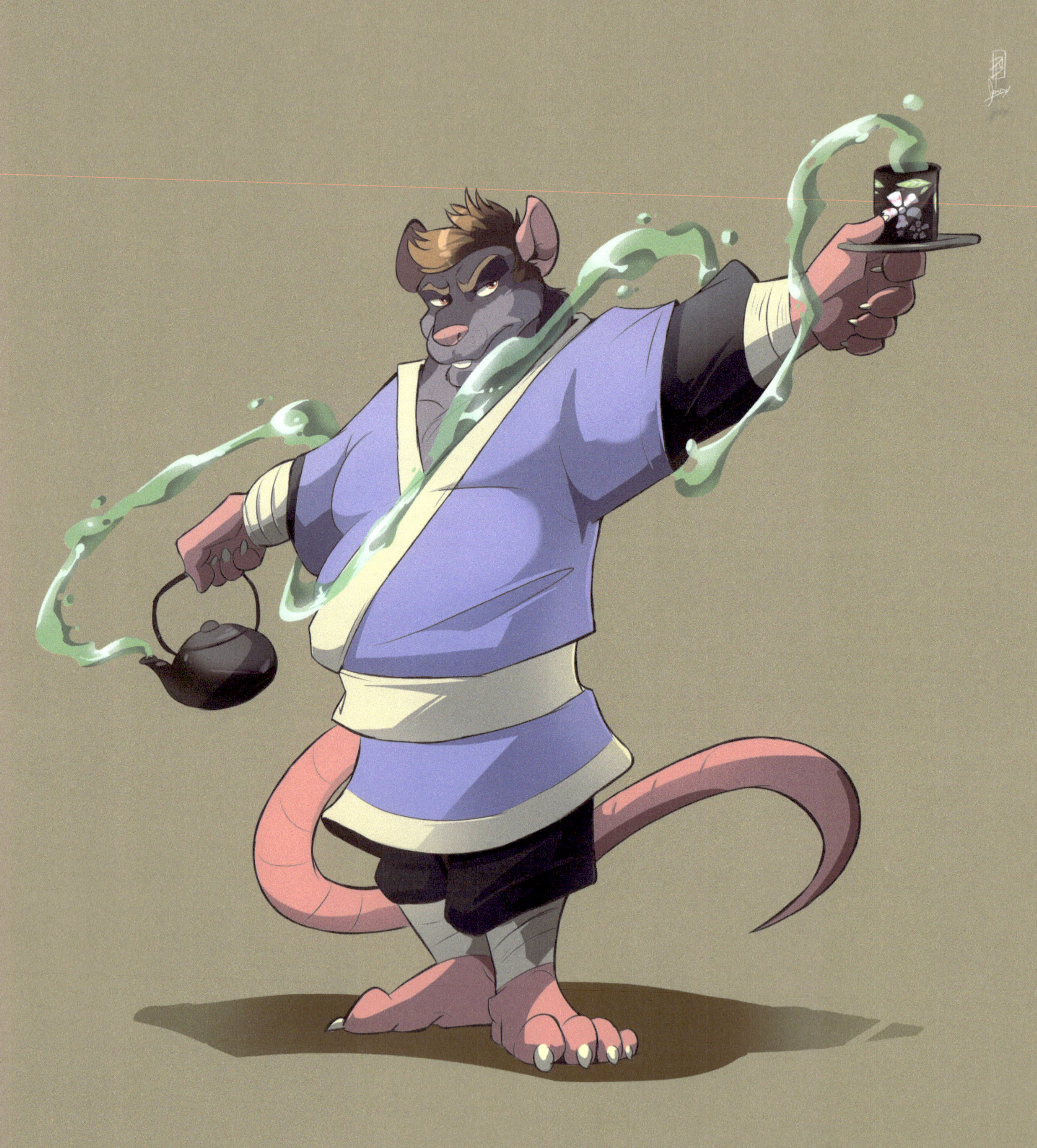

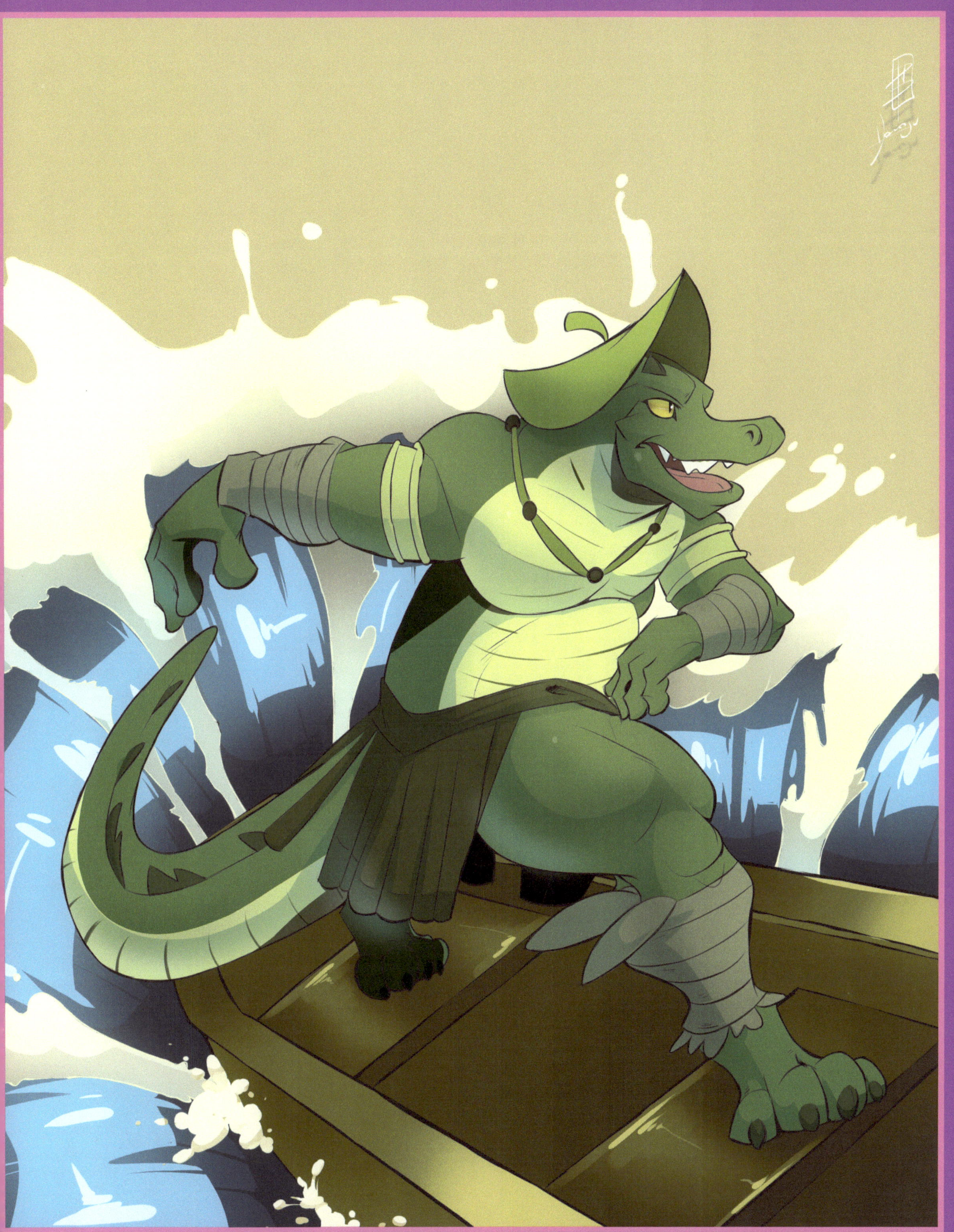

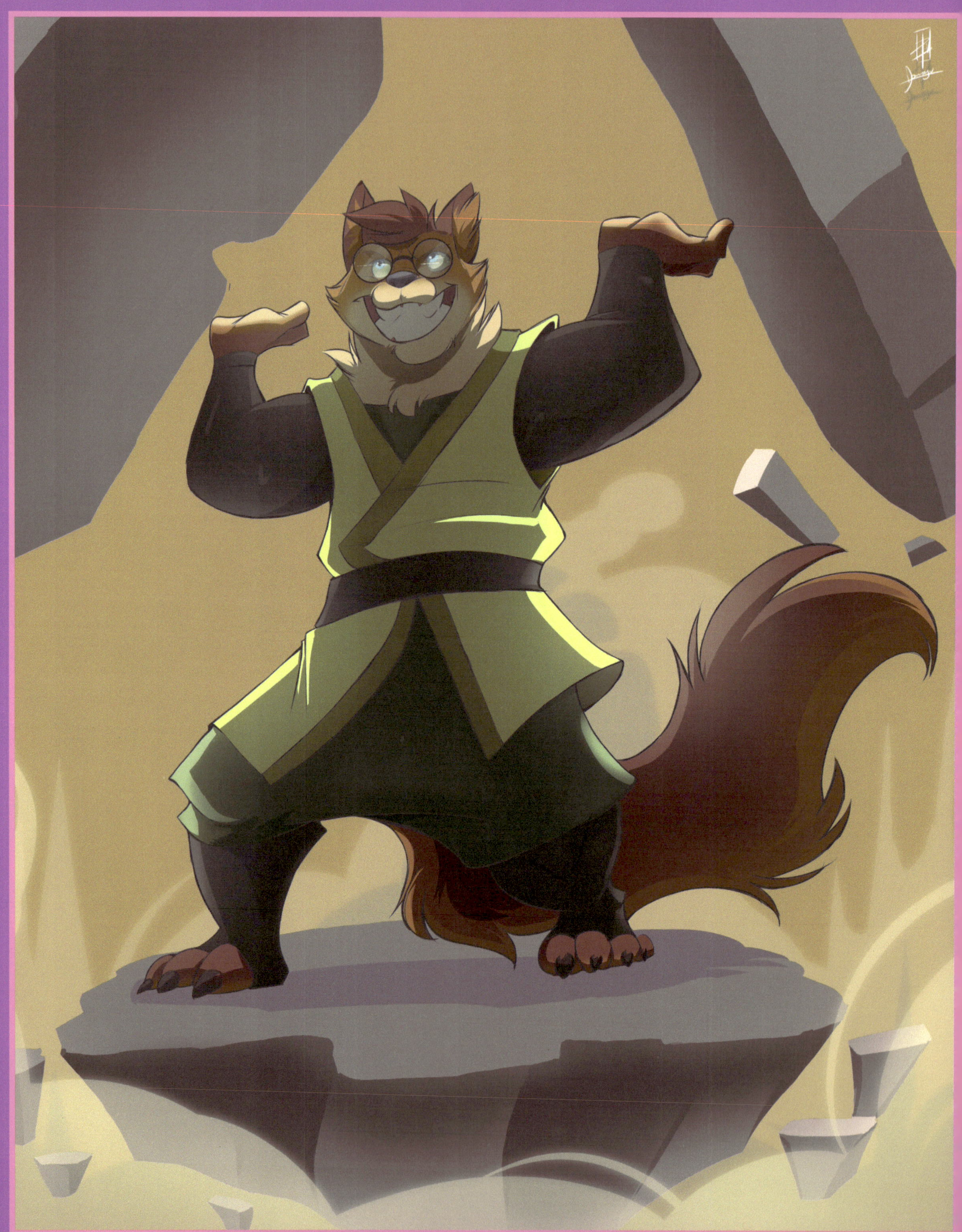

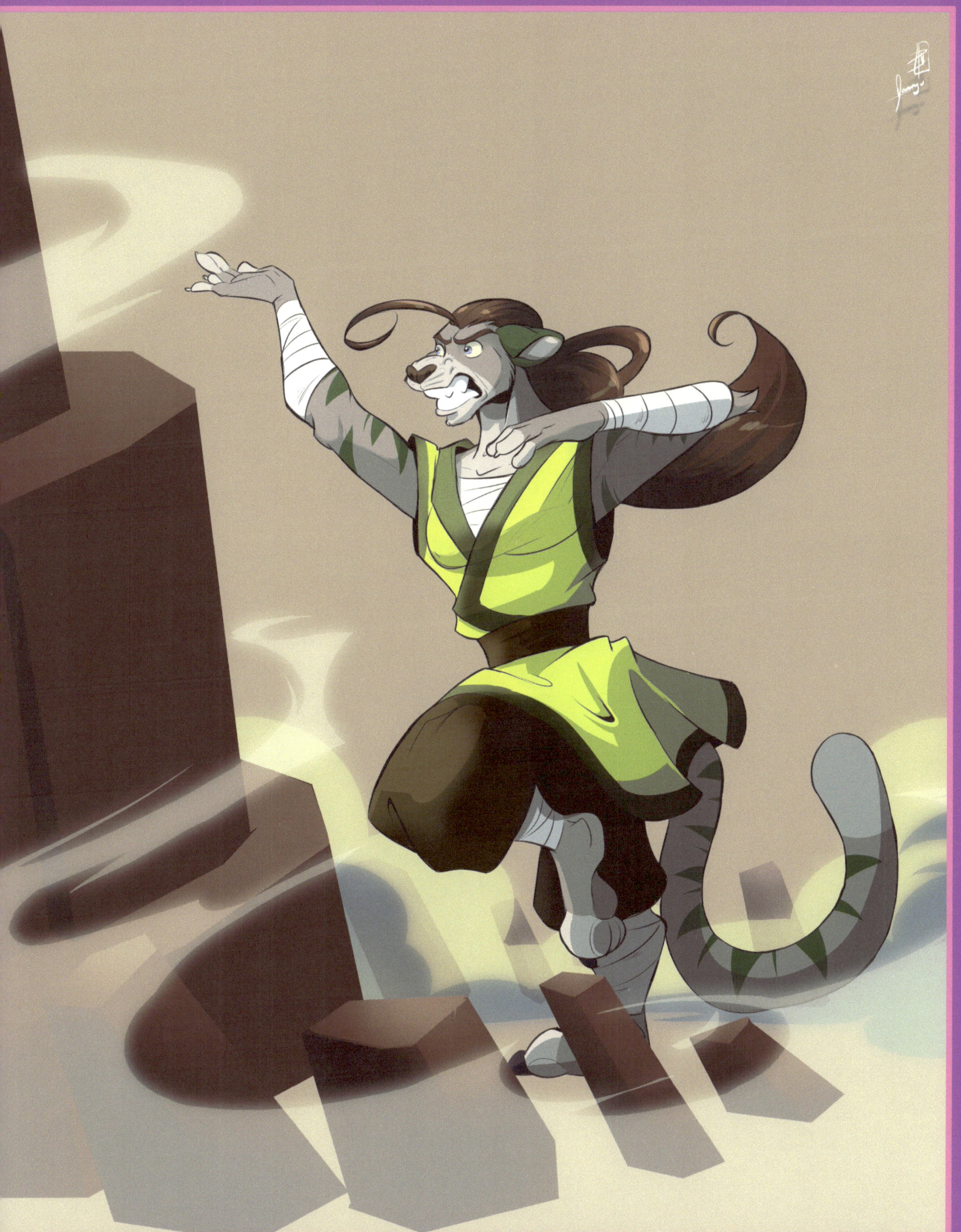

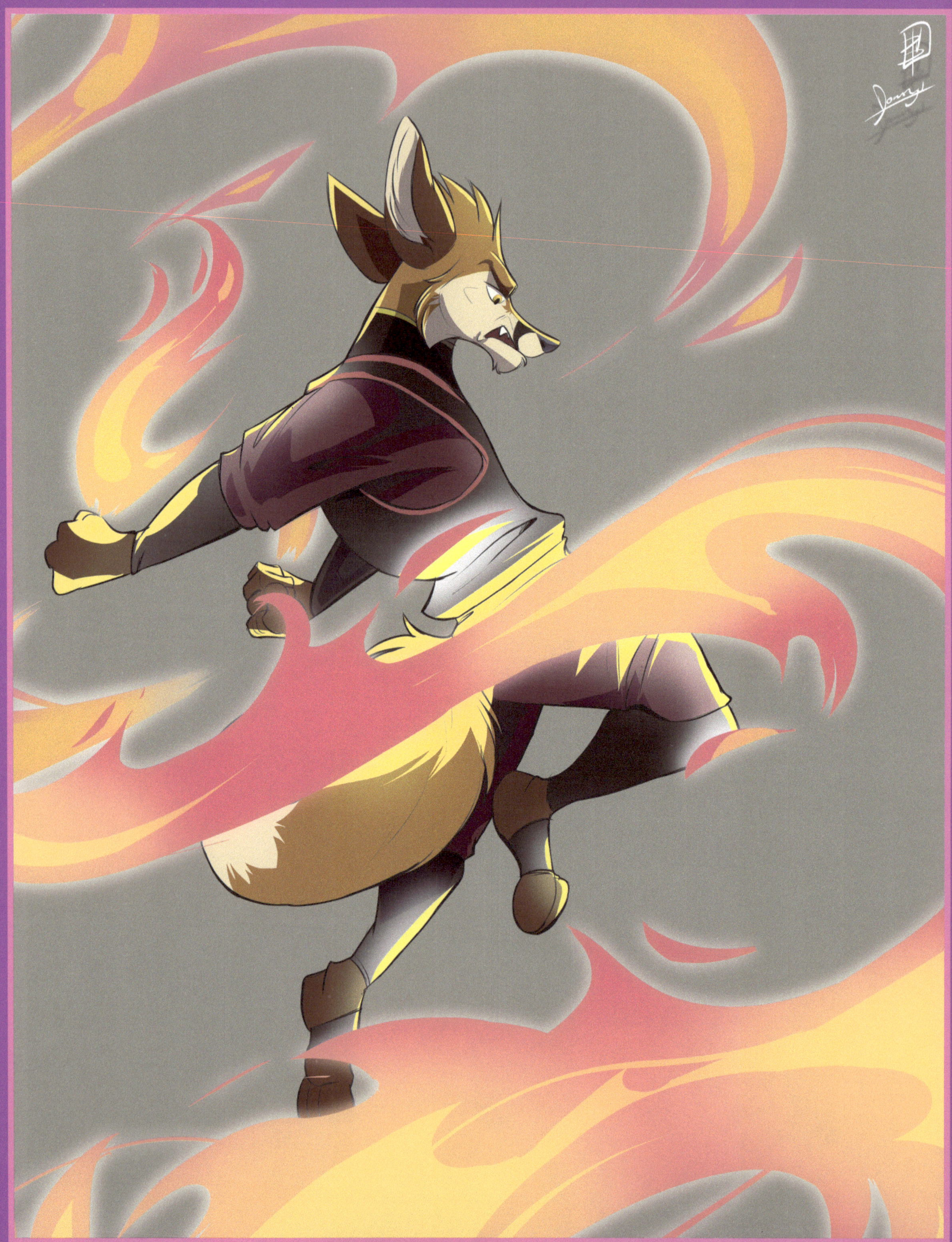

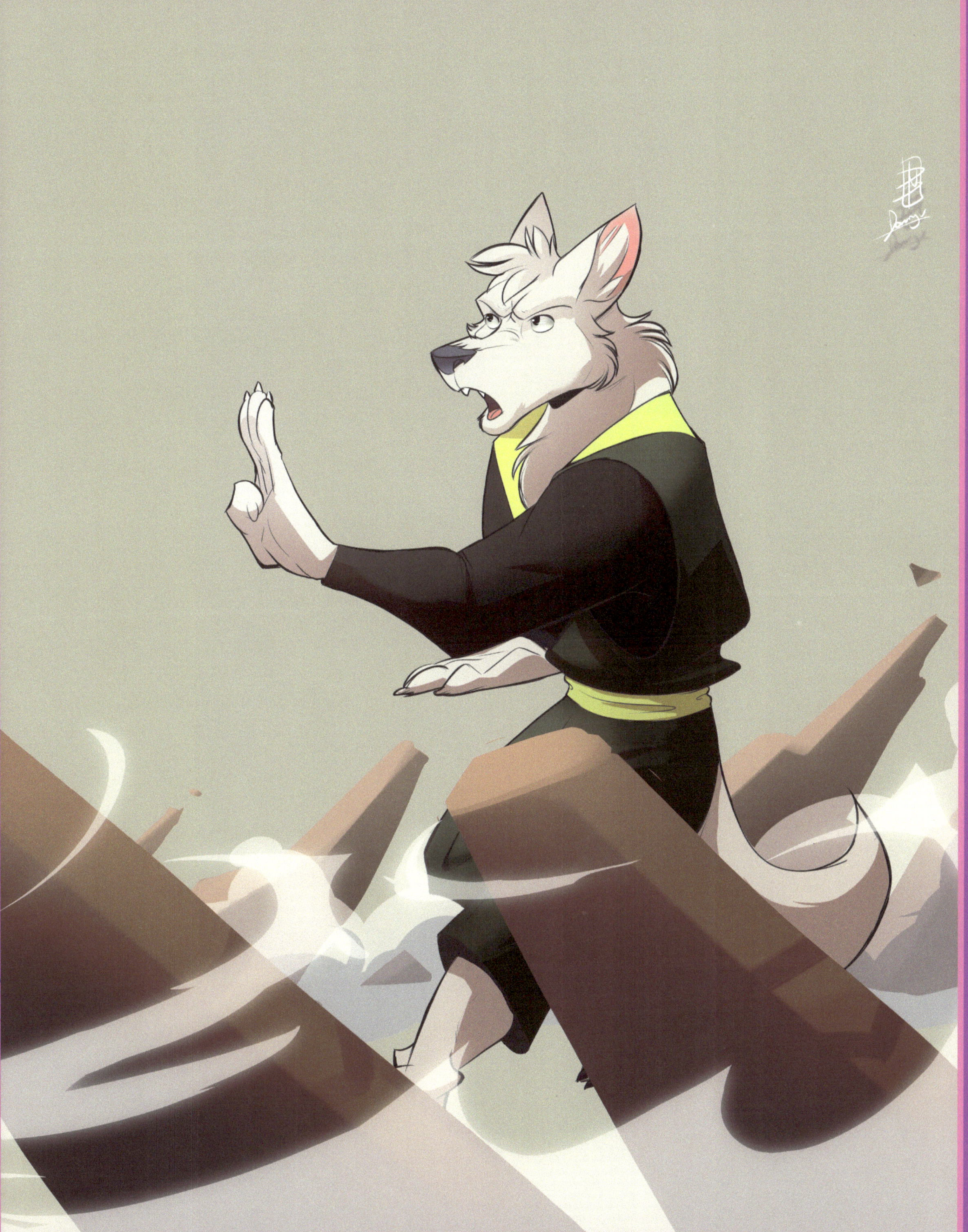

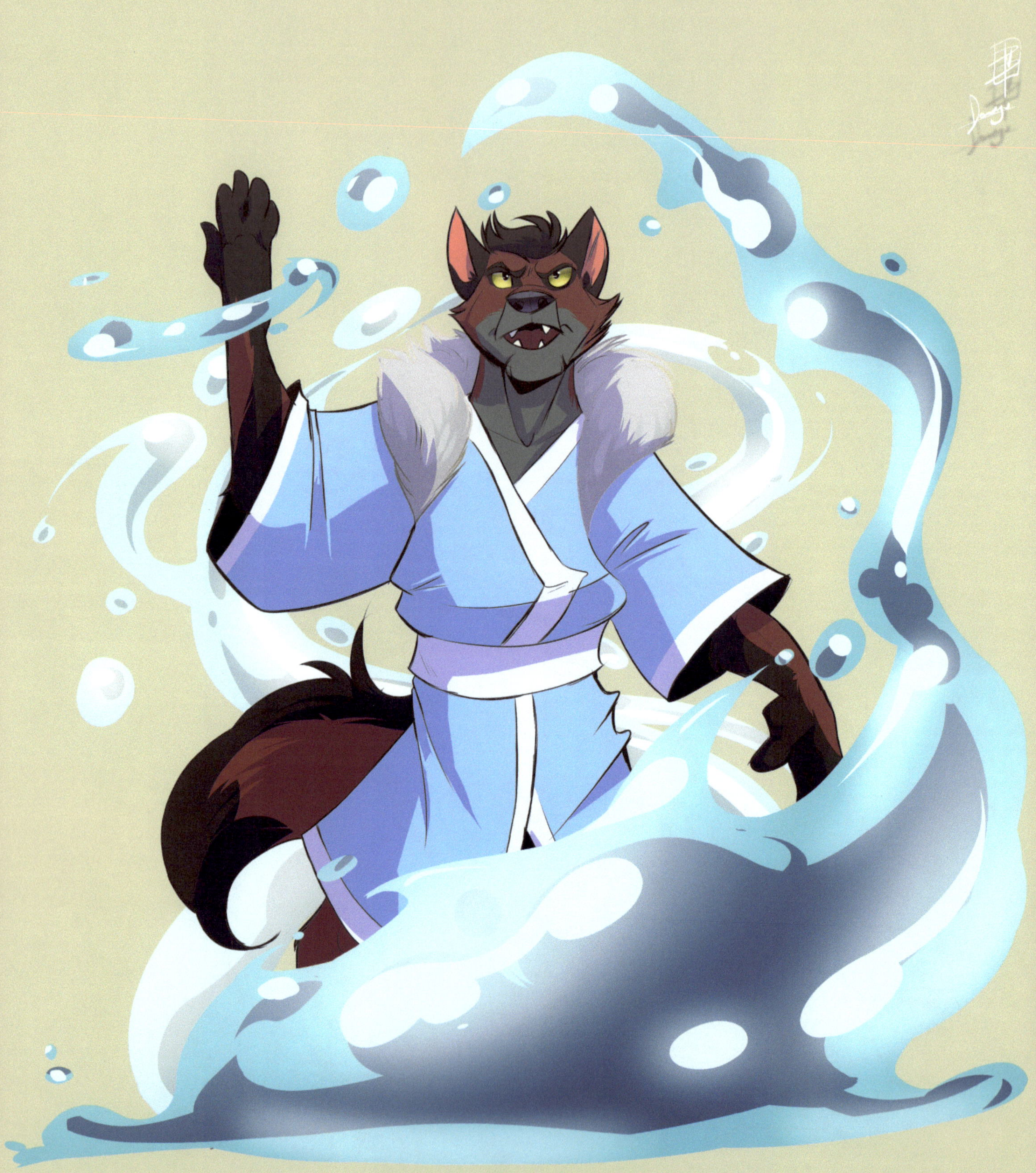

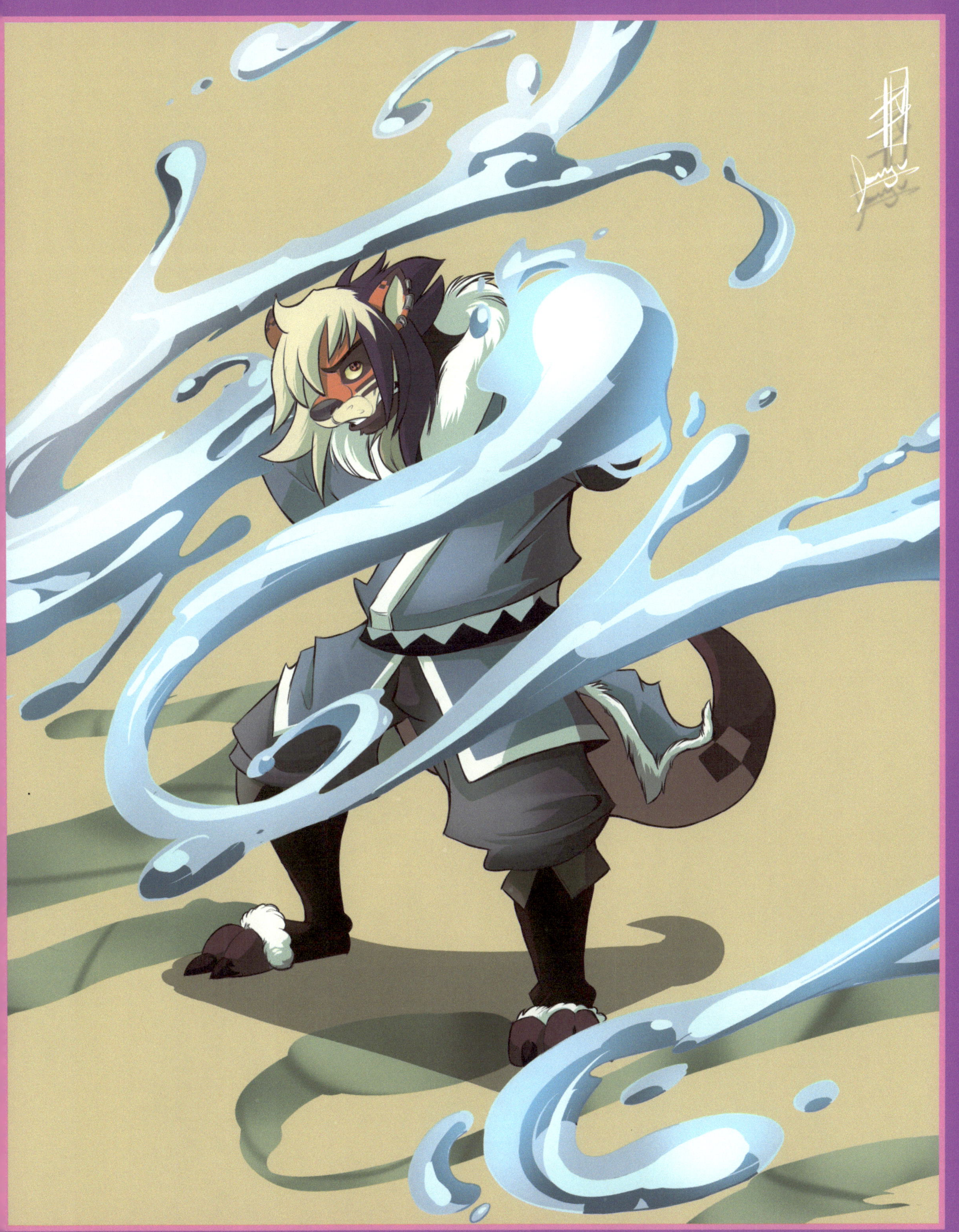

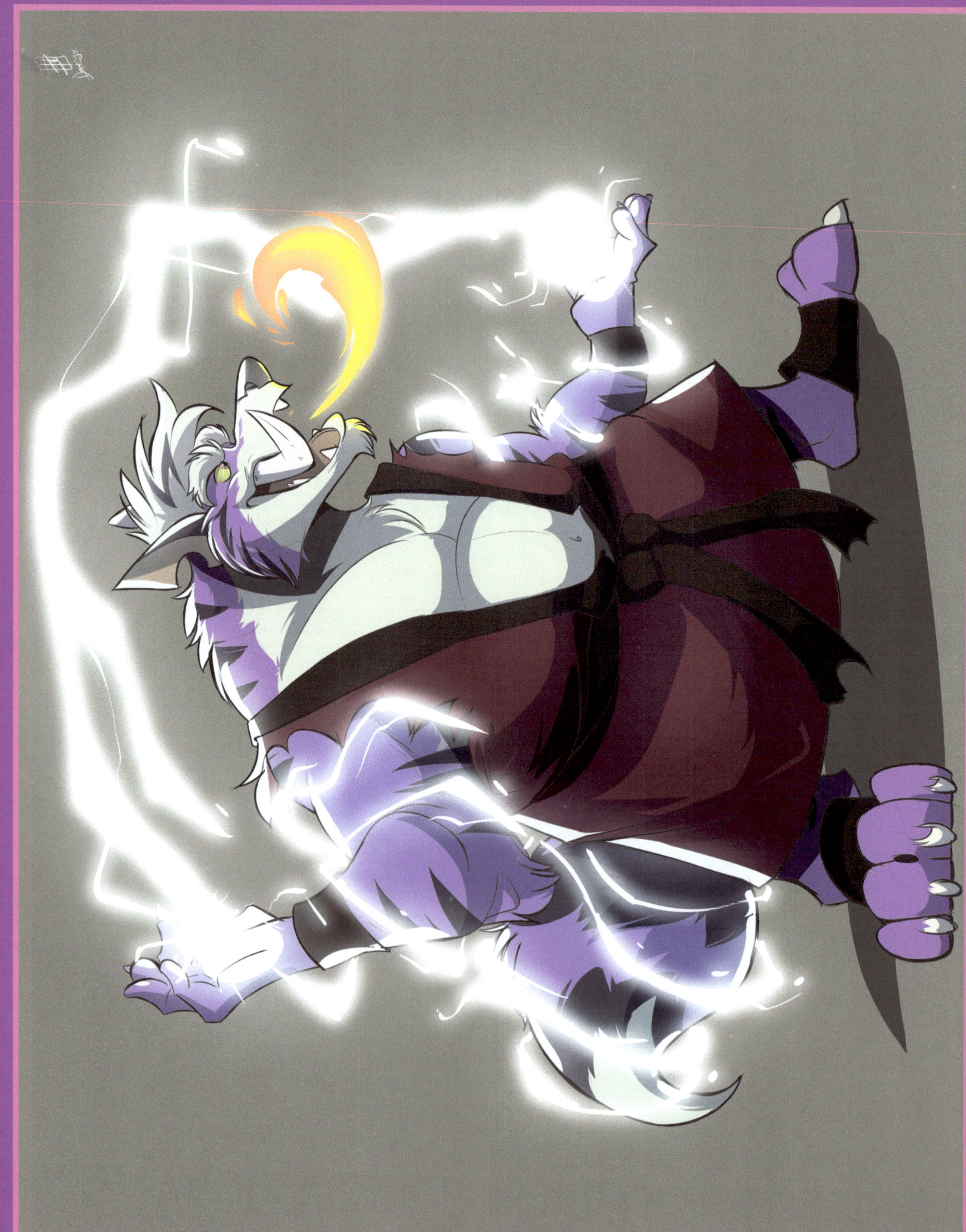

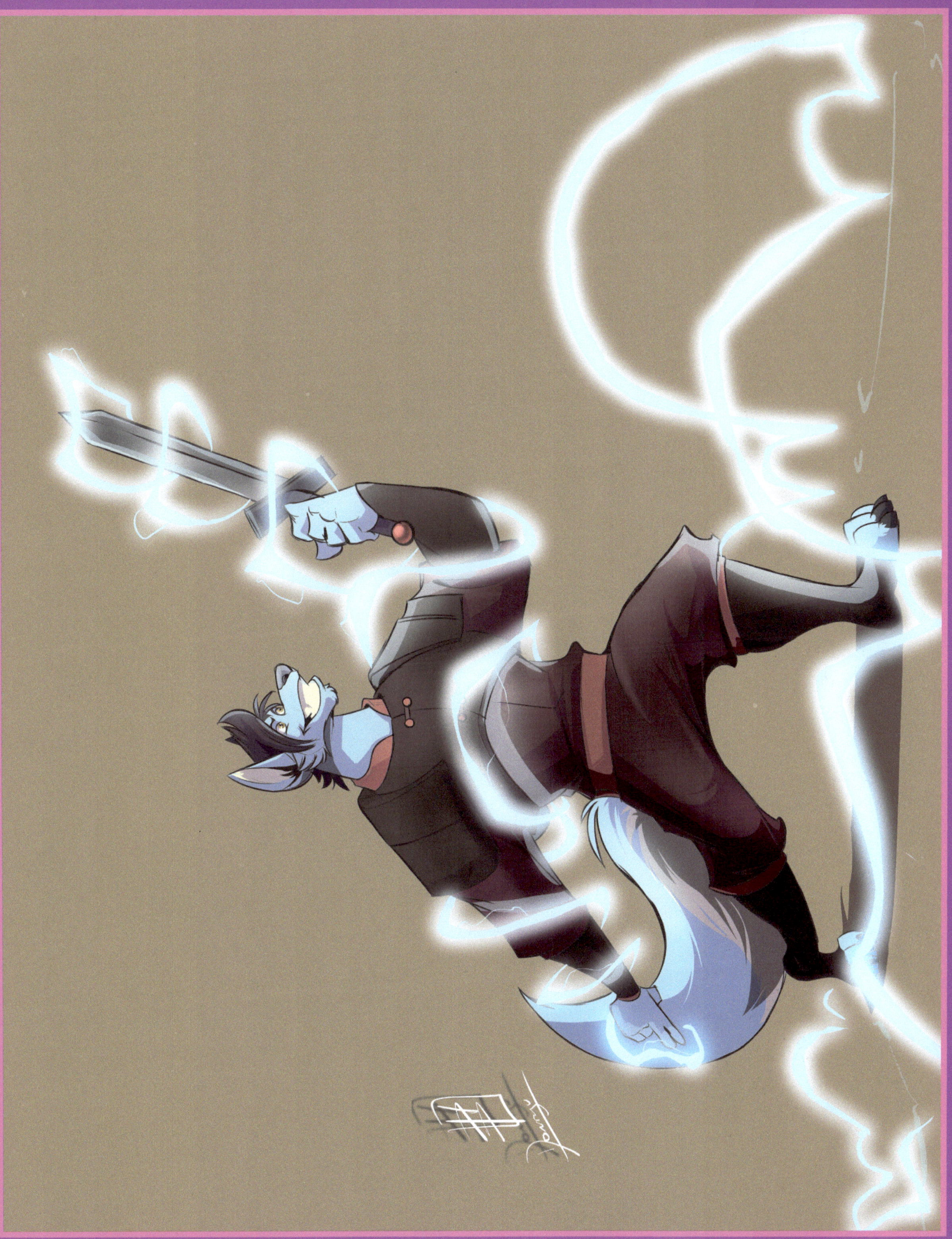

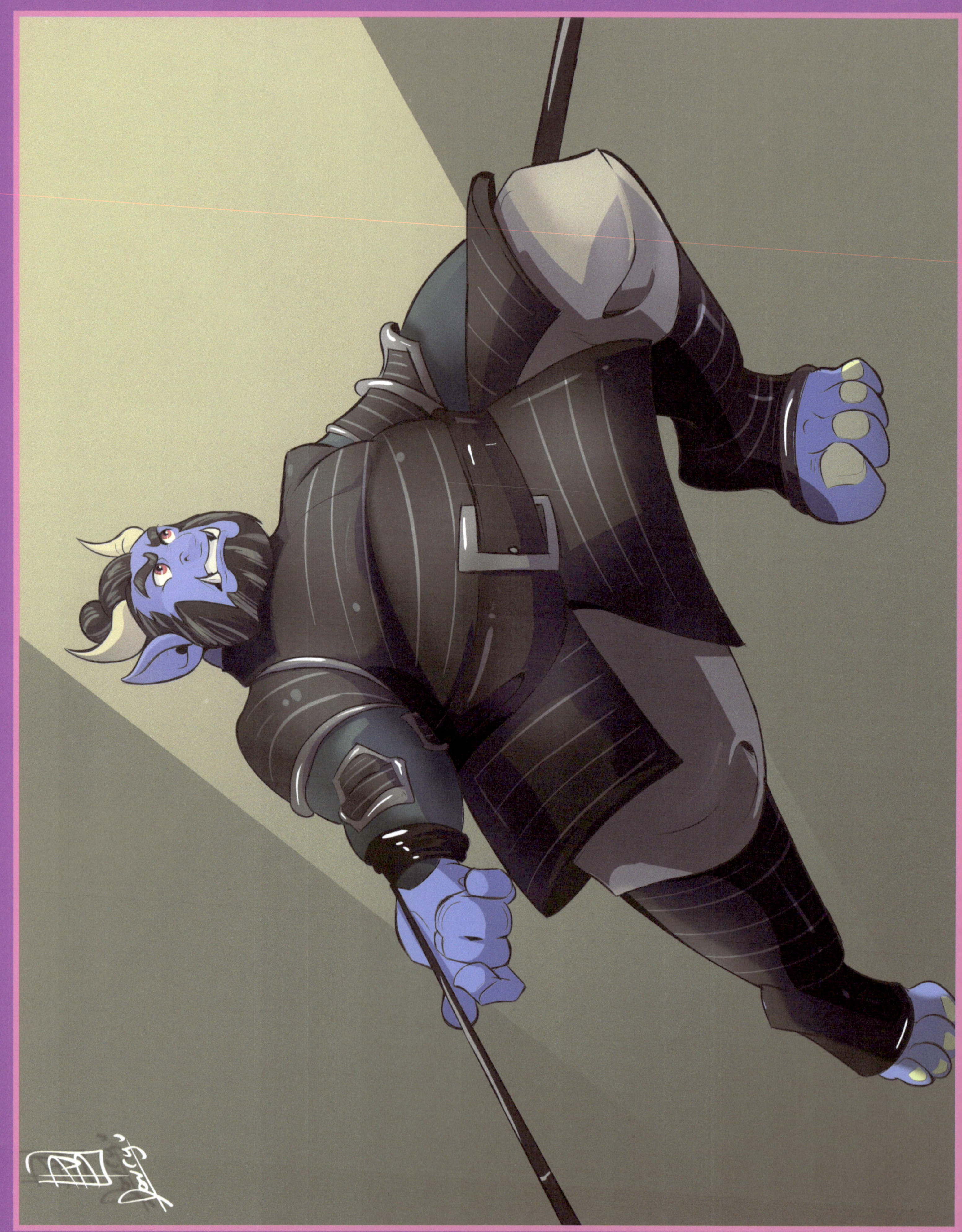

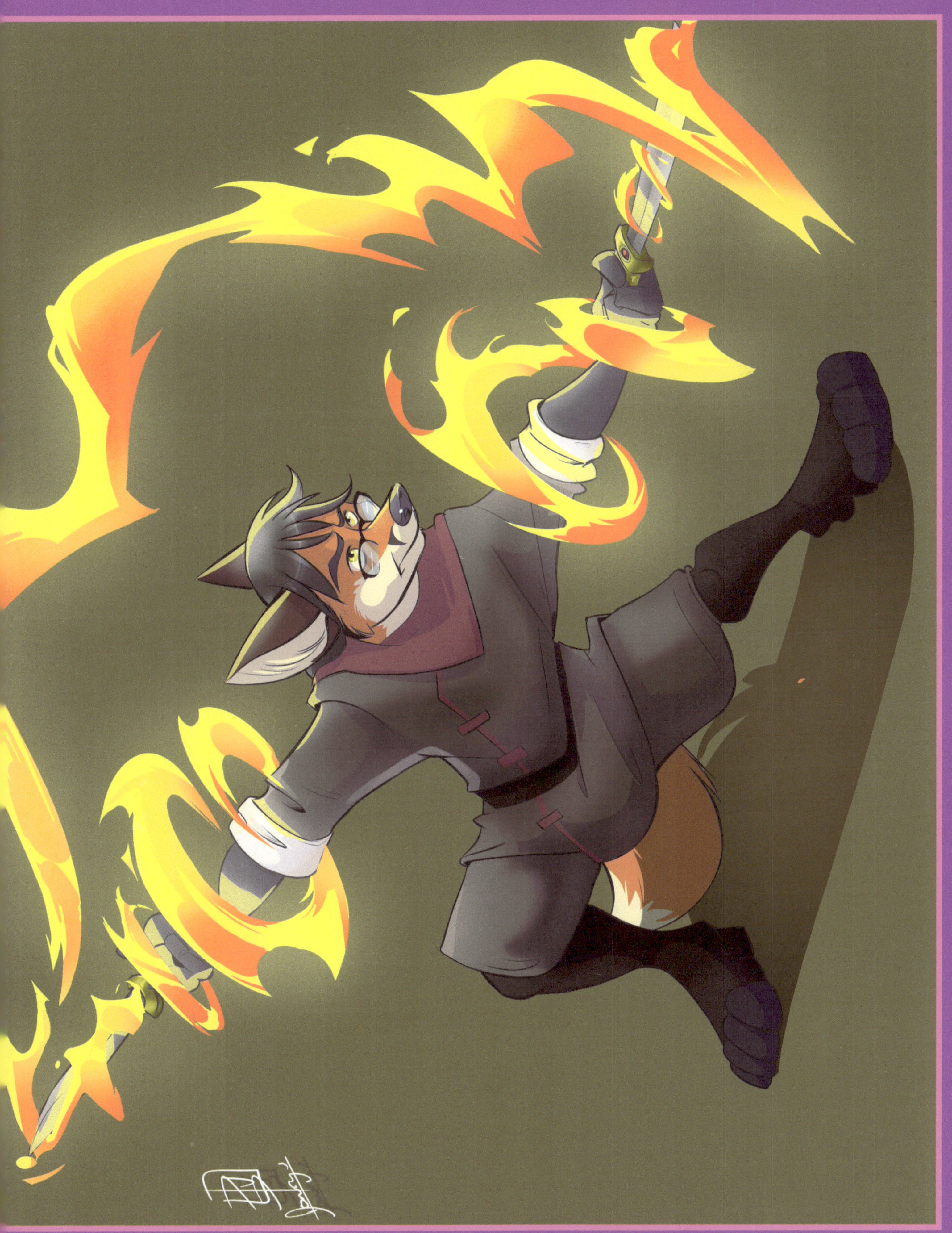

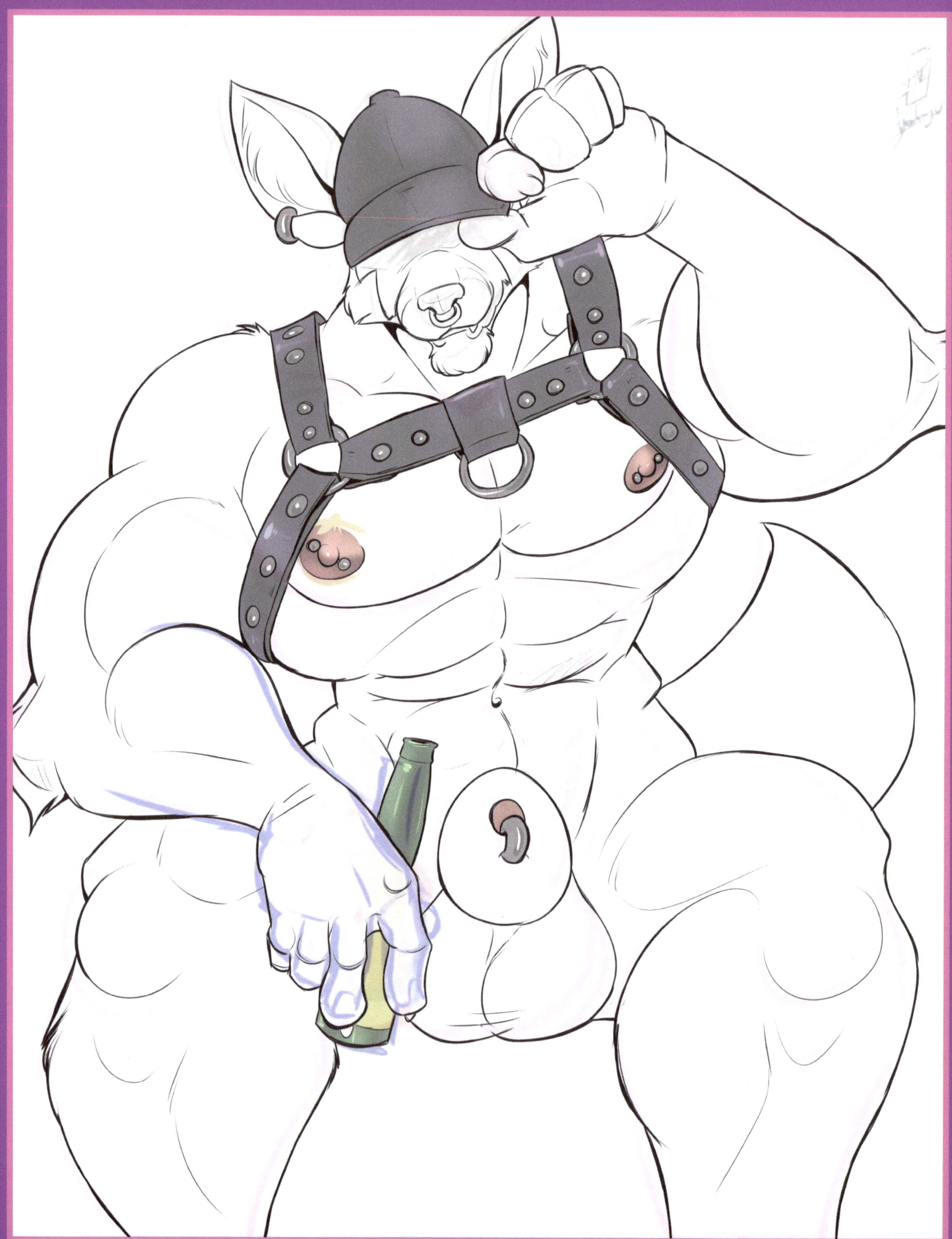

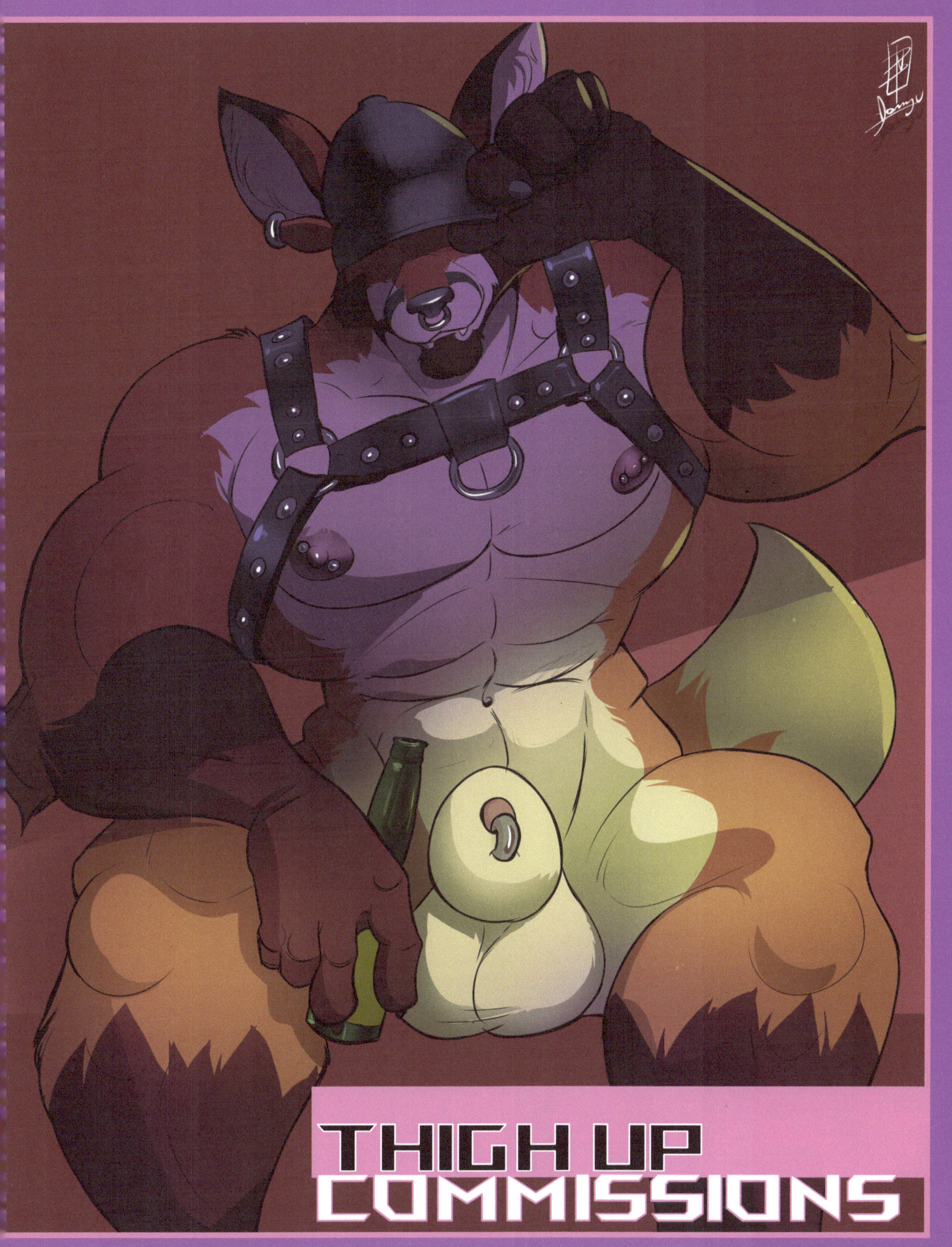
THIGH UP
COMMISSIONS

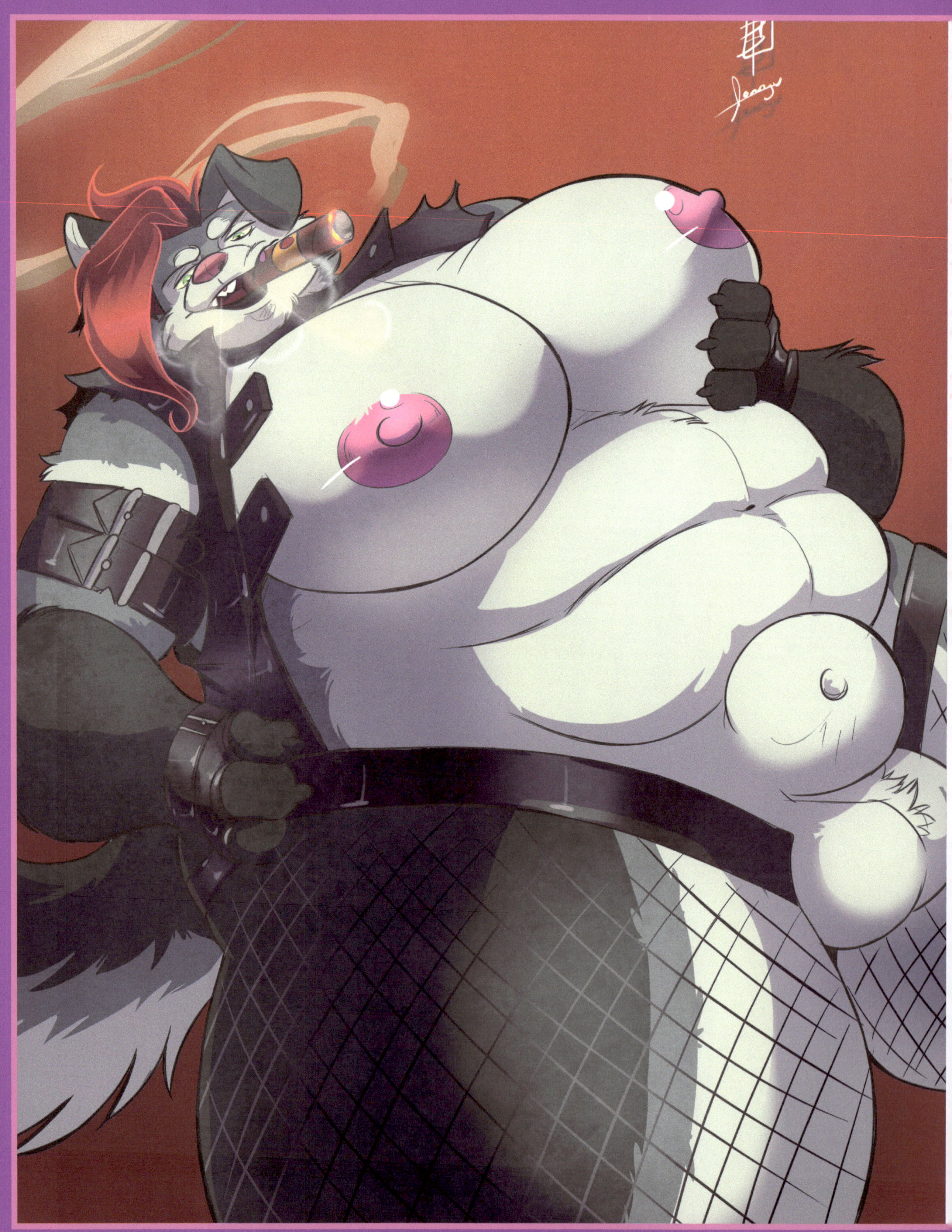

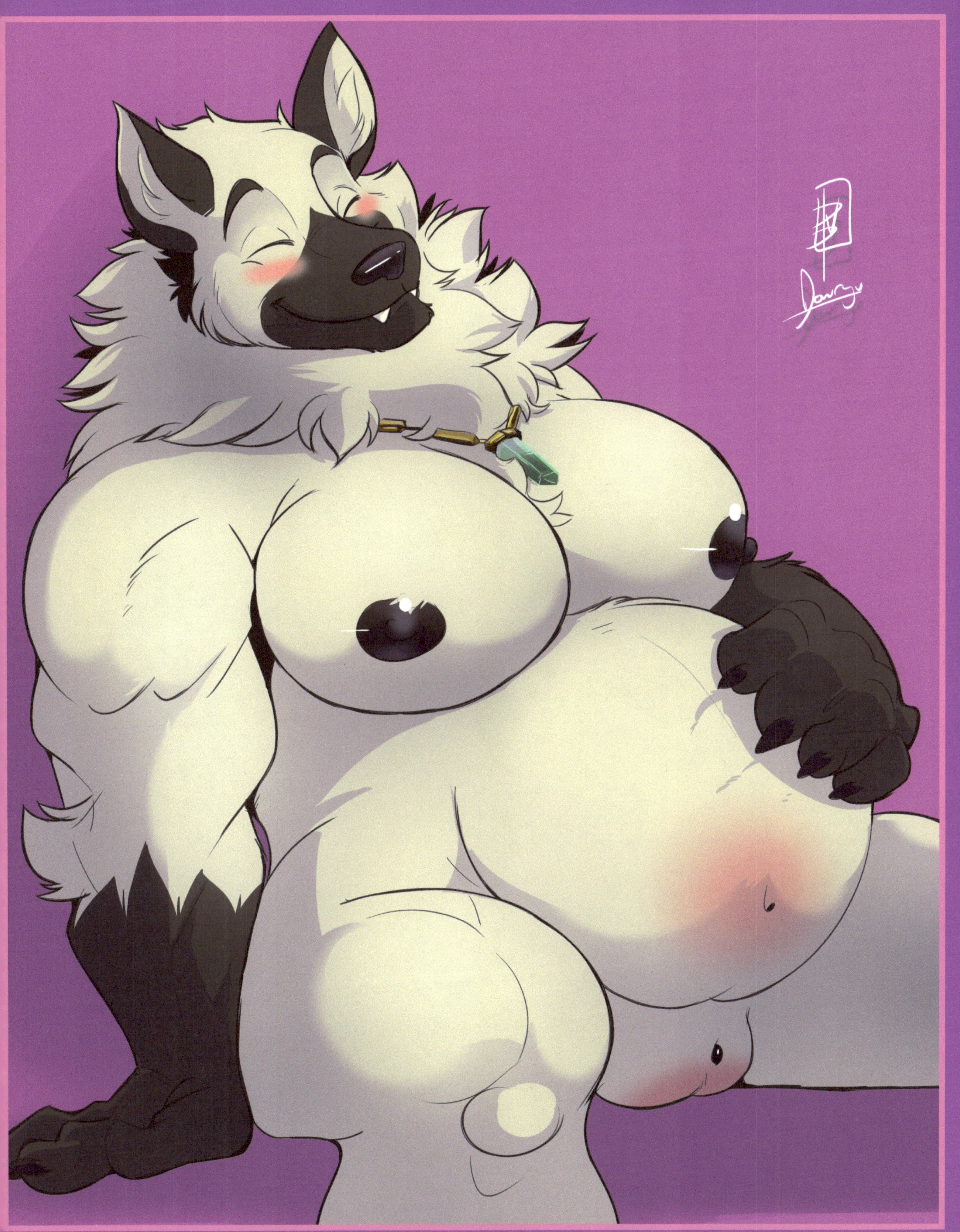

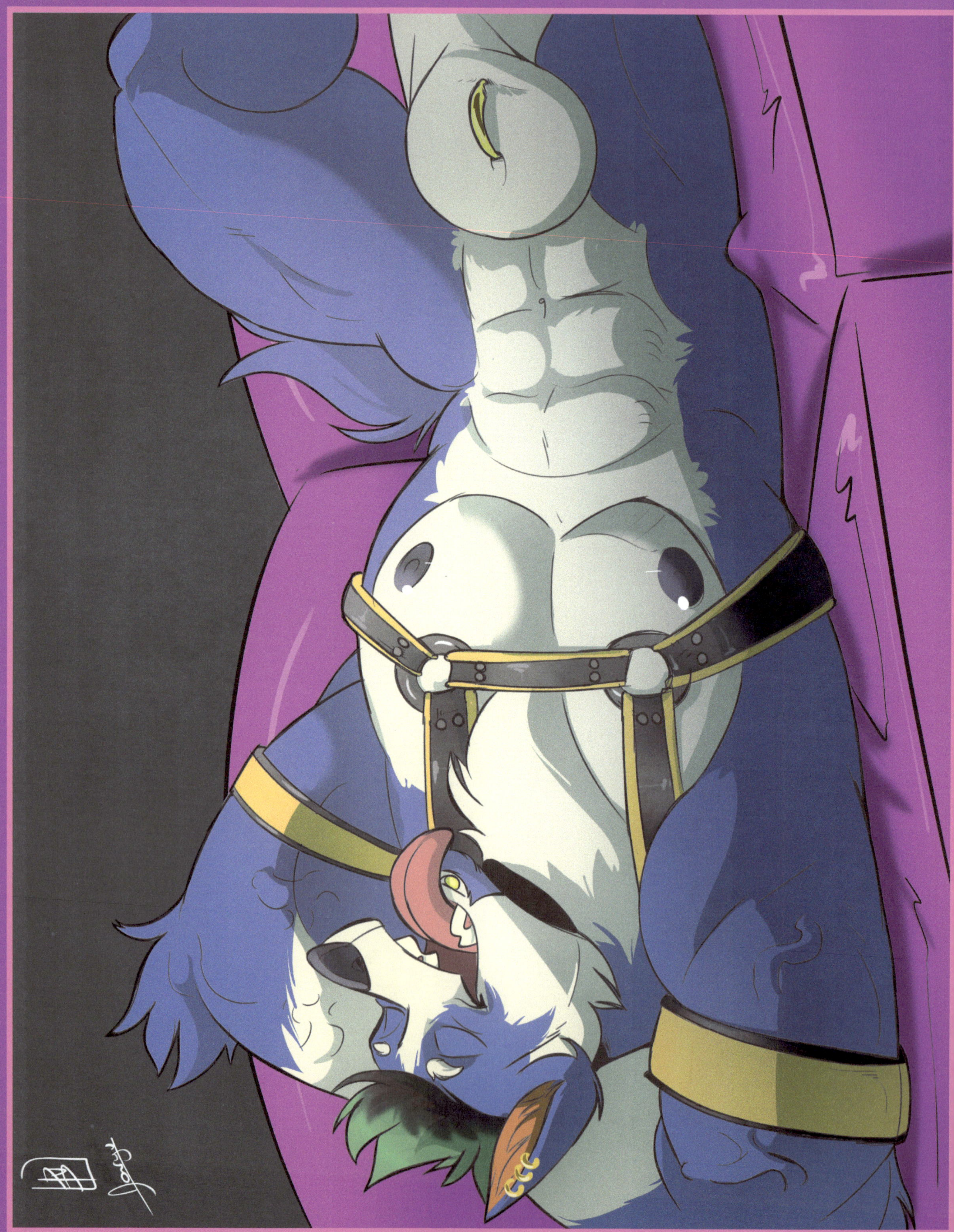

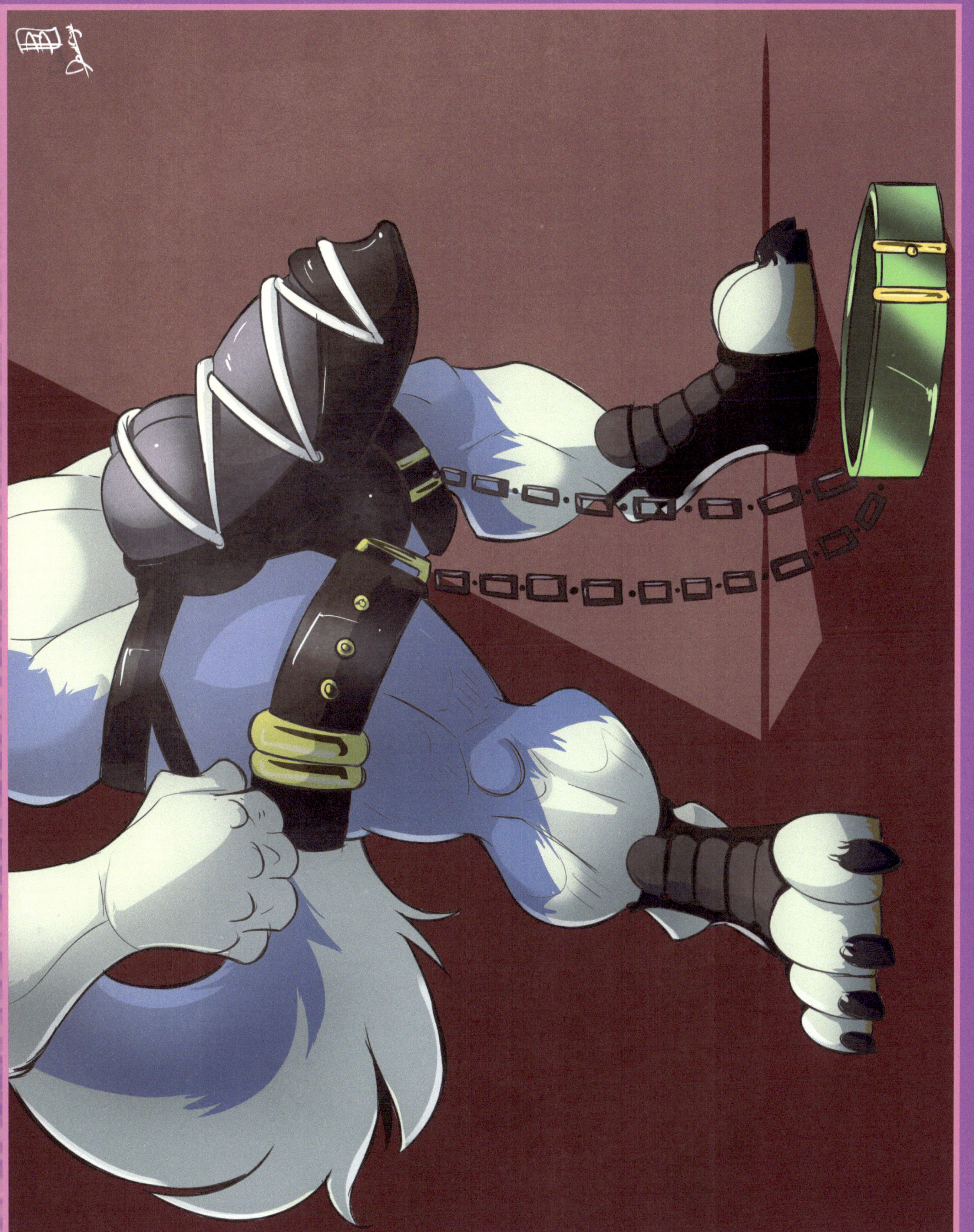

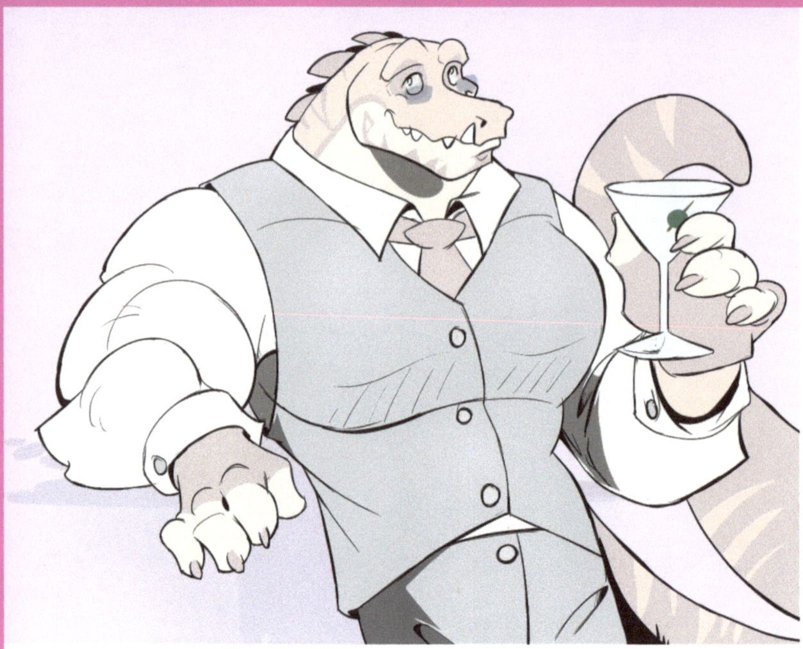

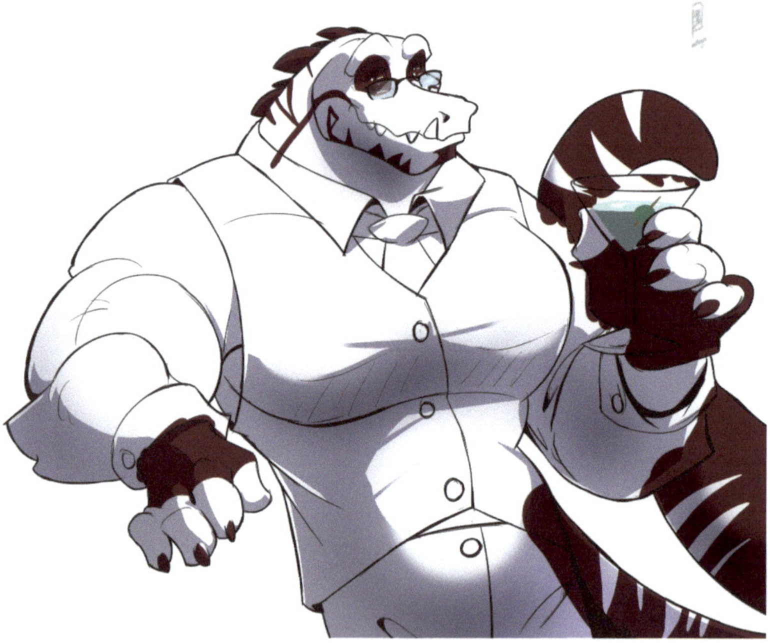

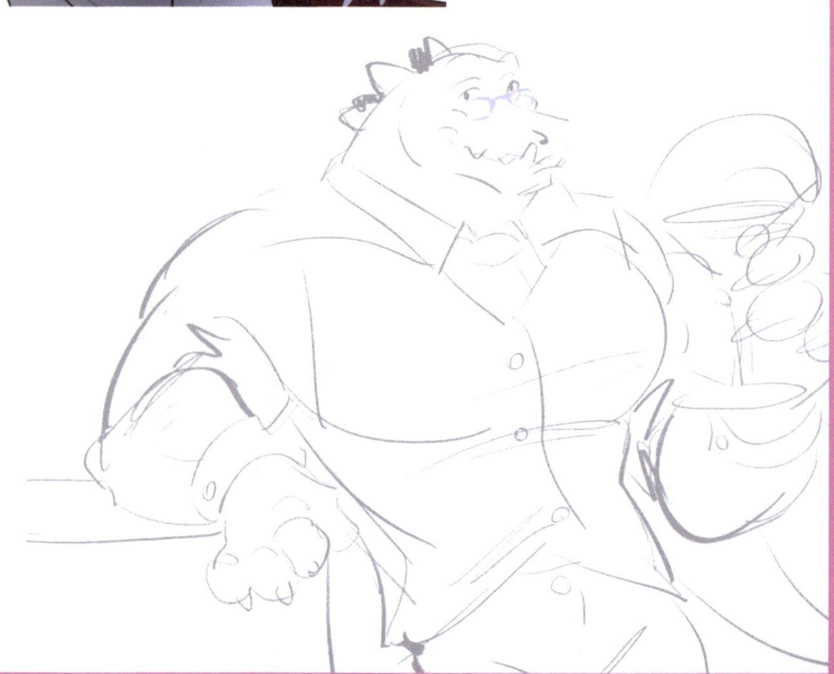

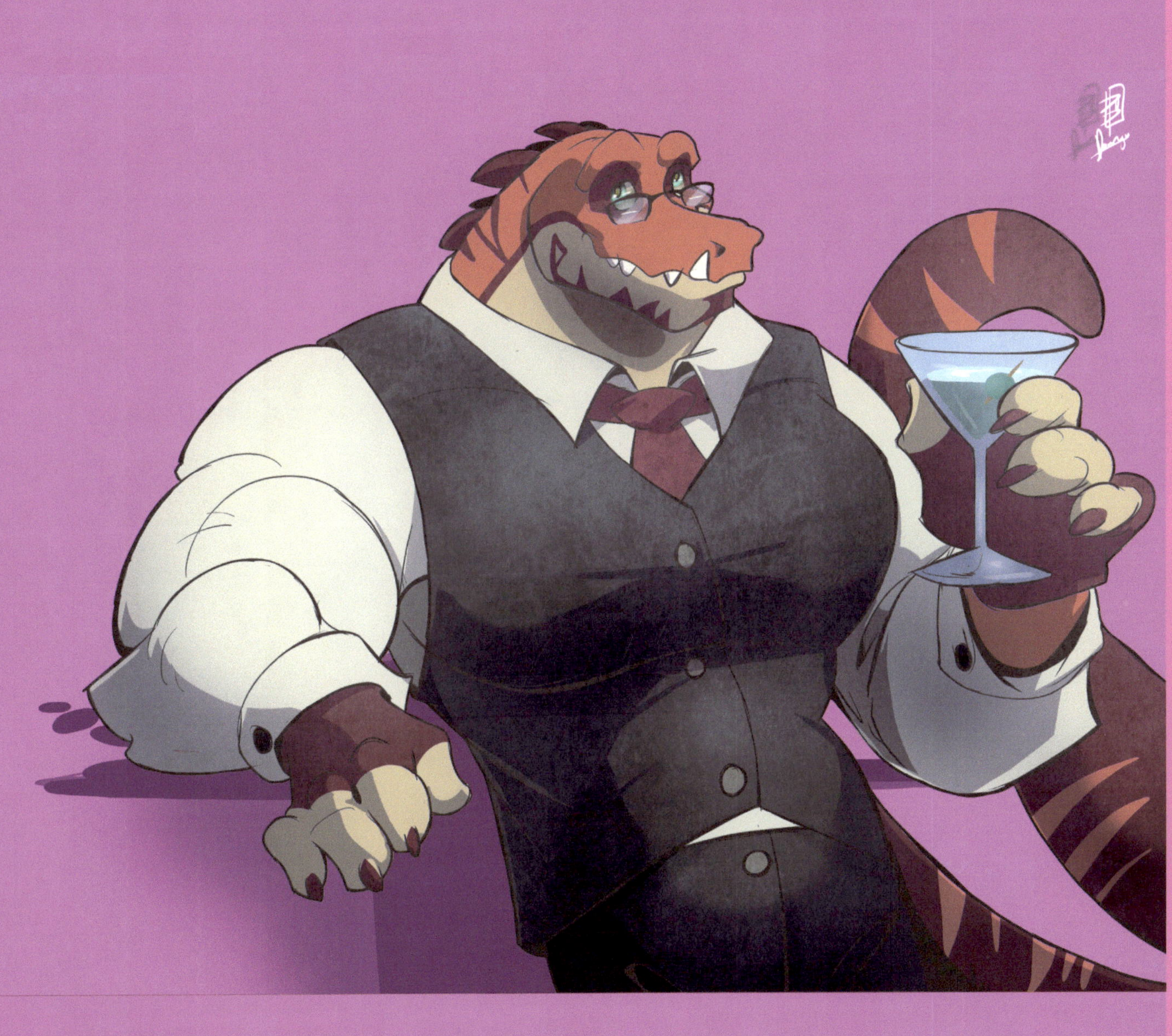

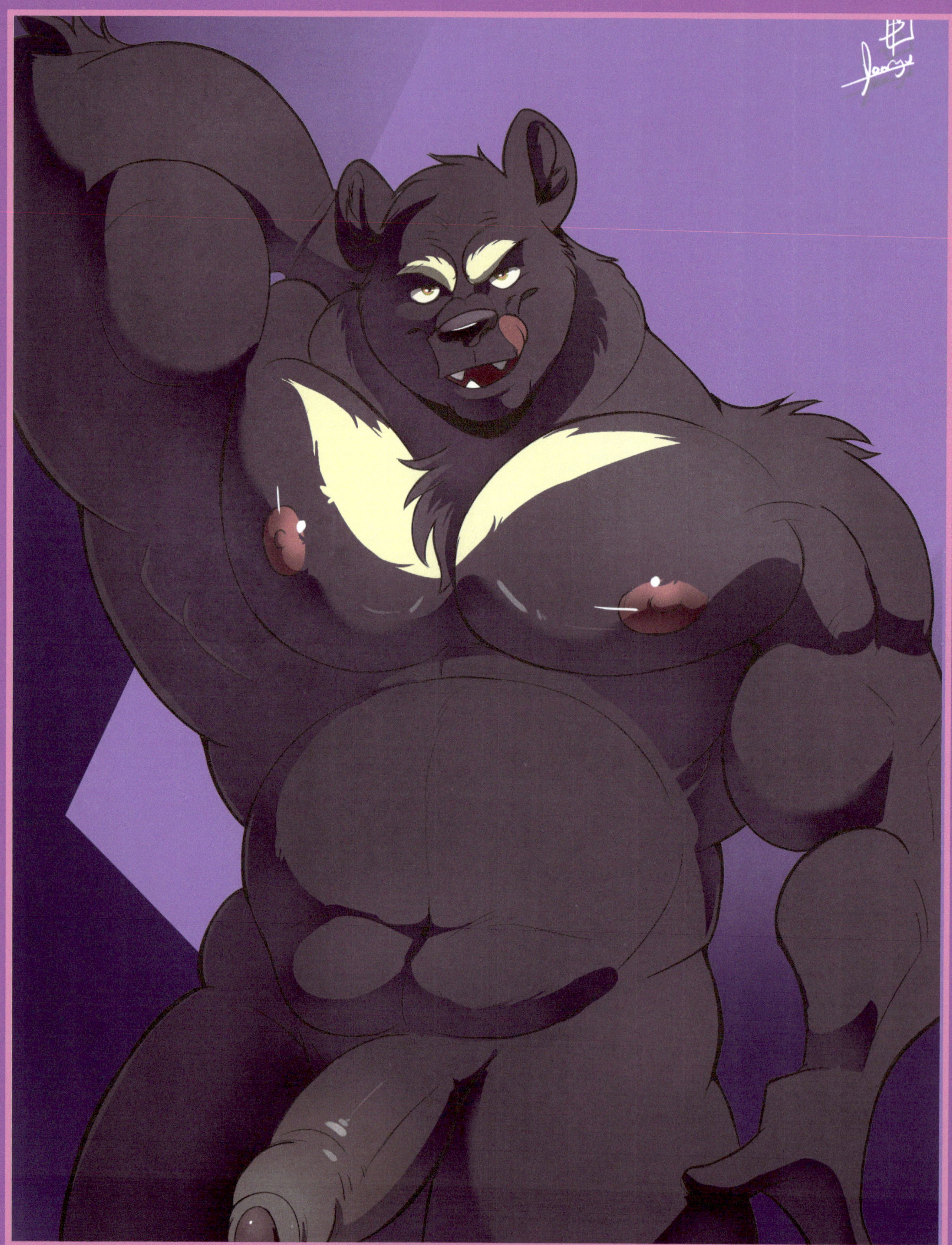

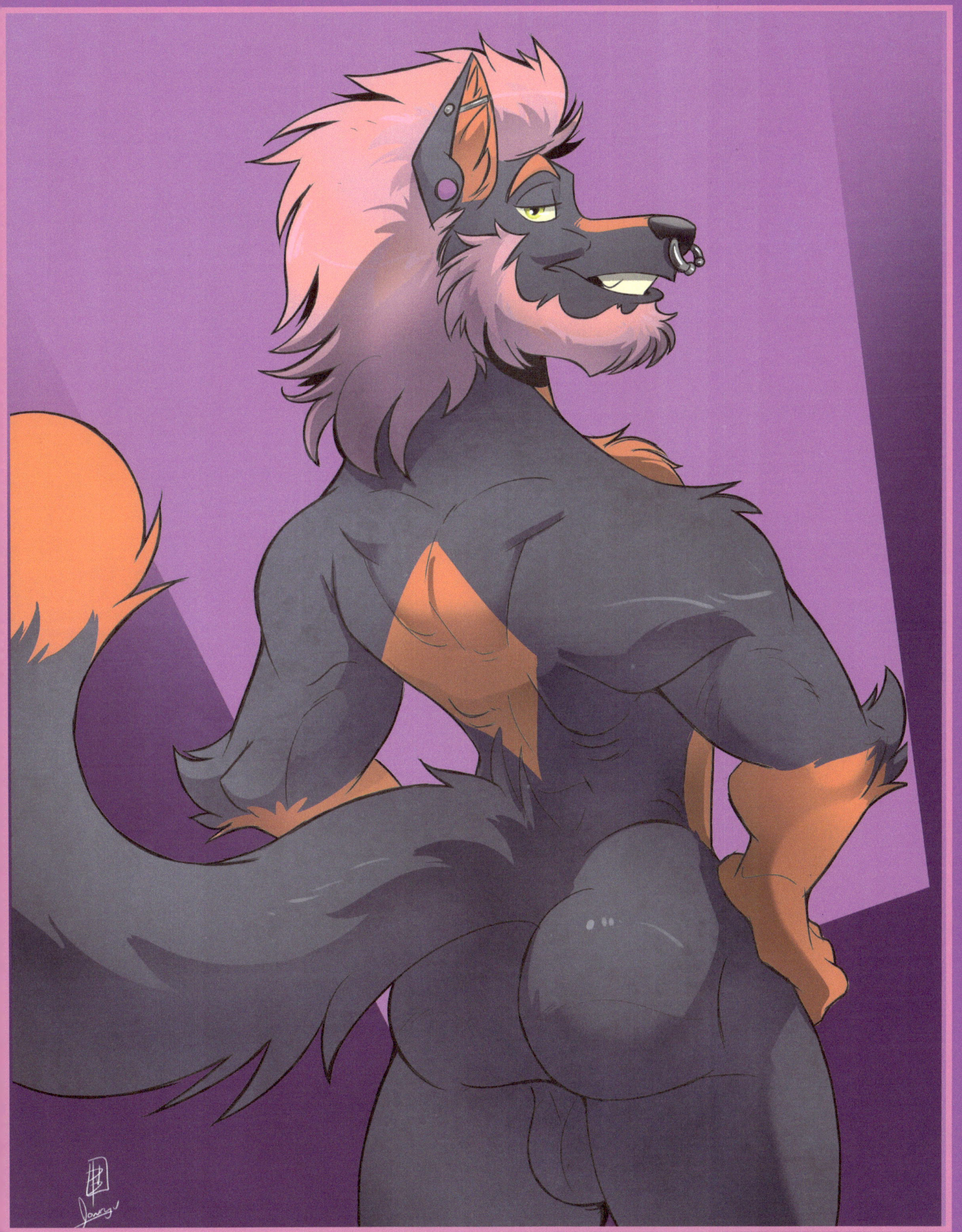

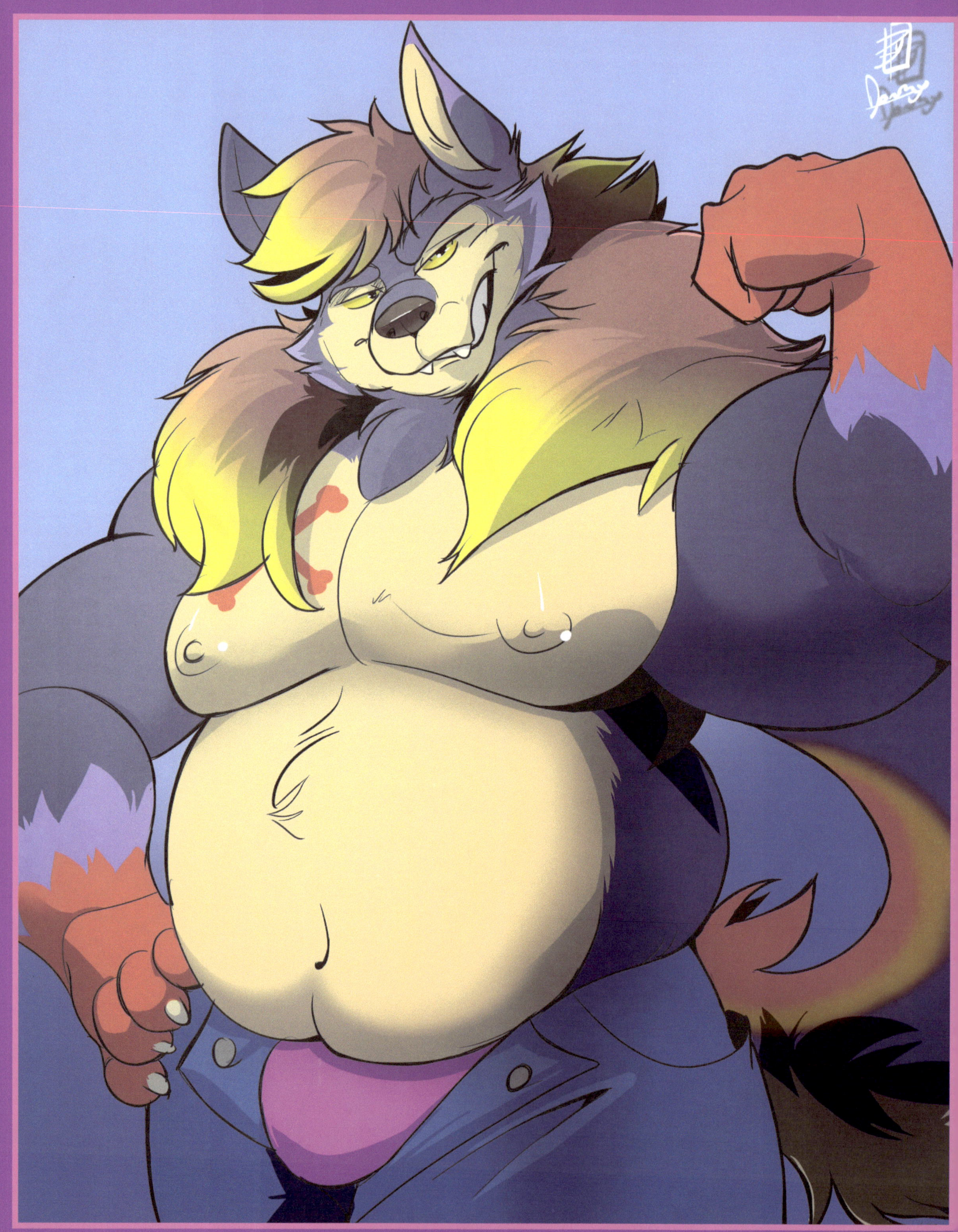

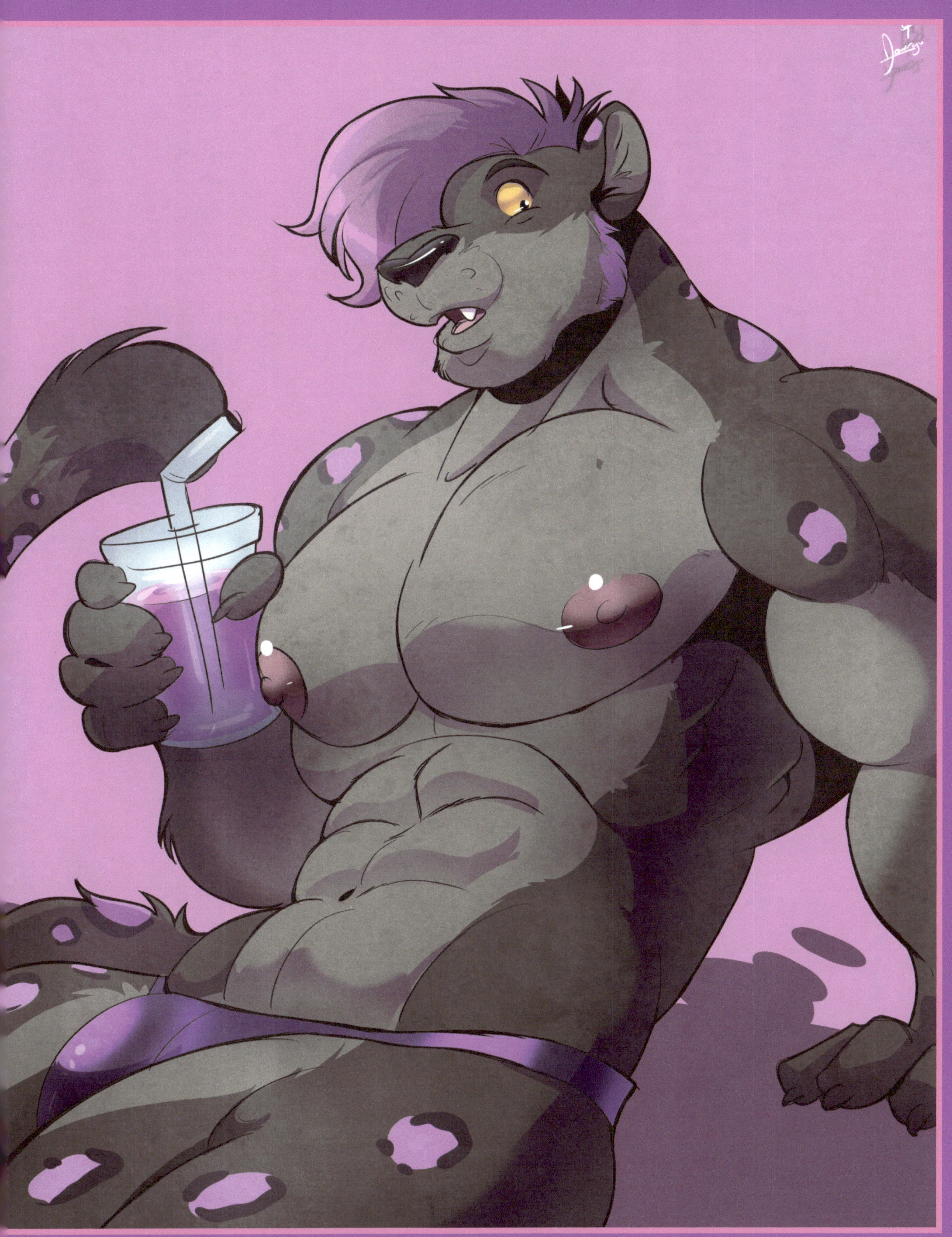

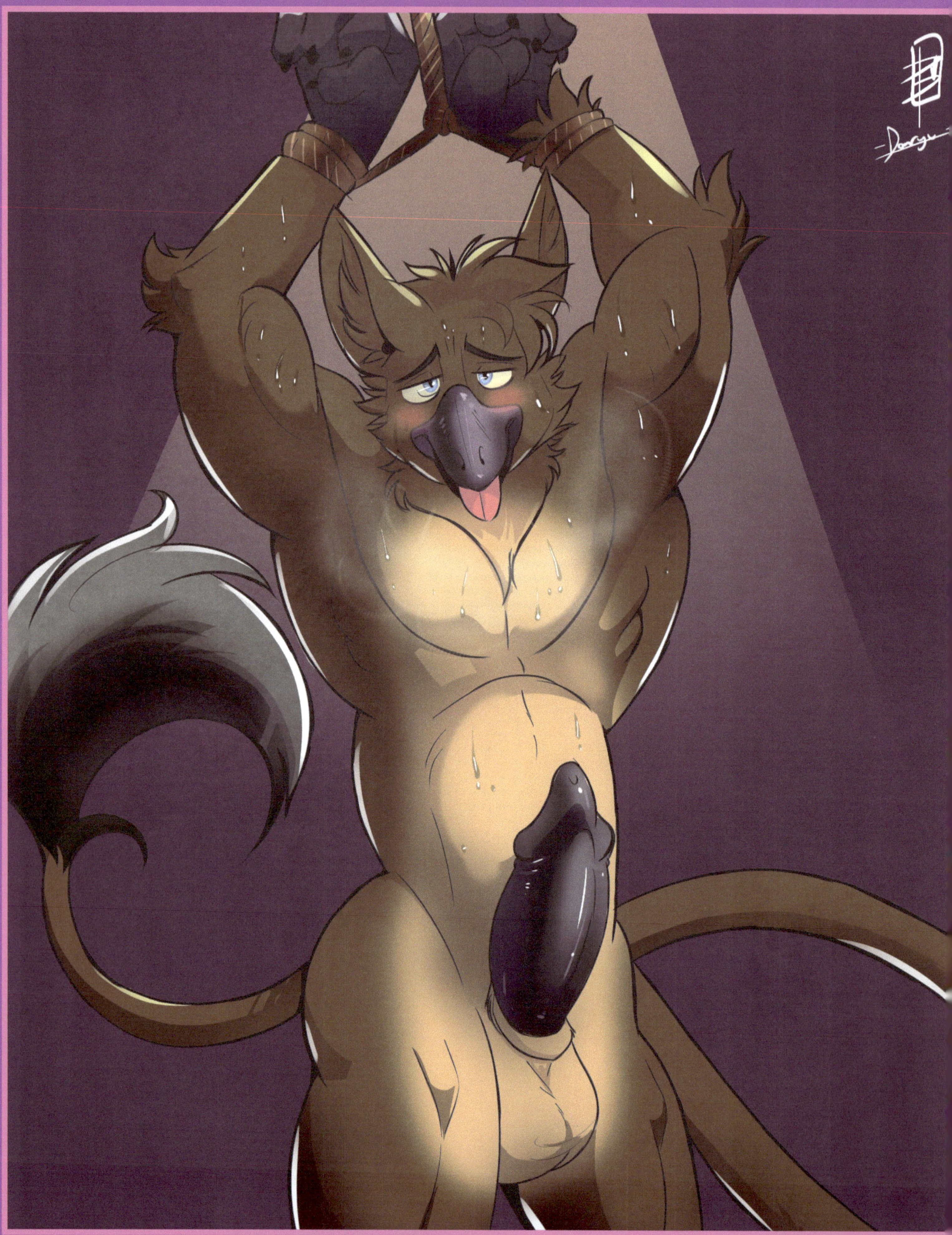

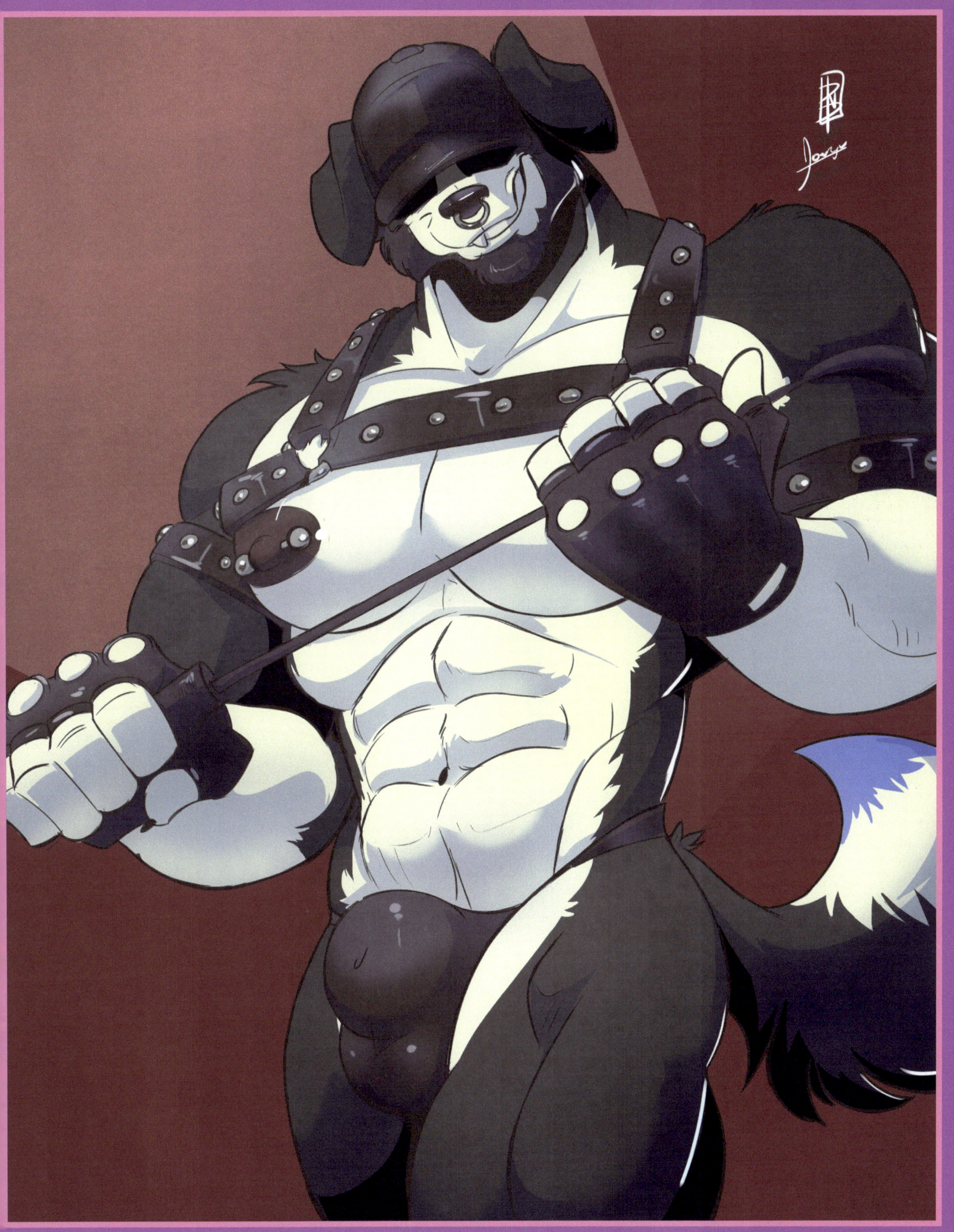

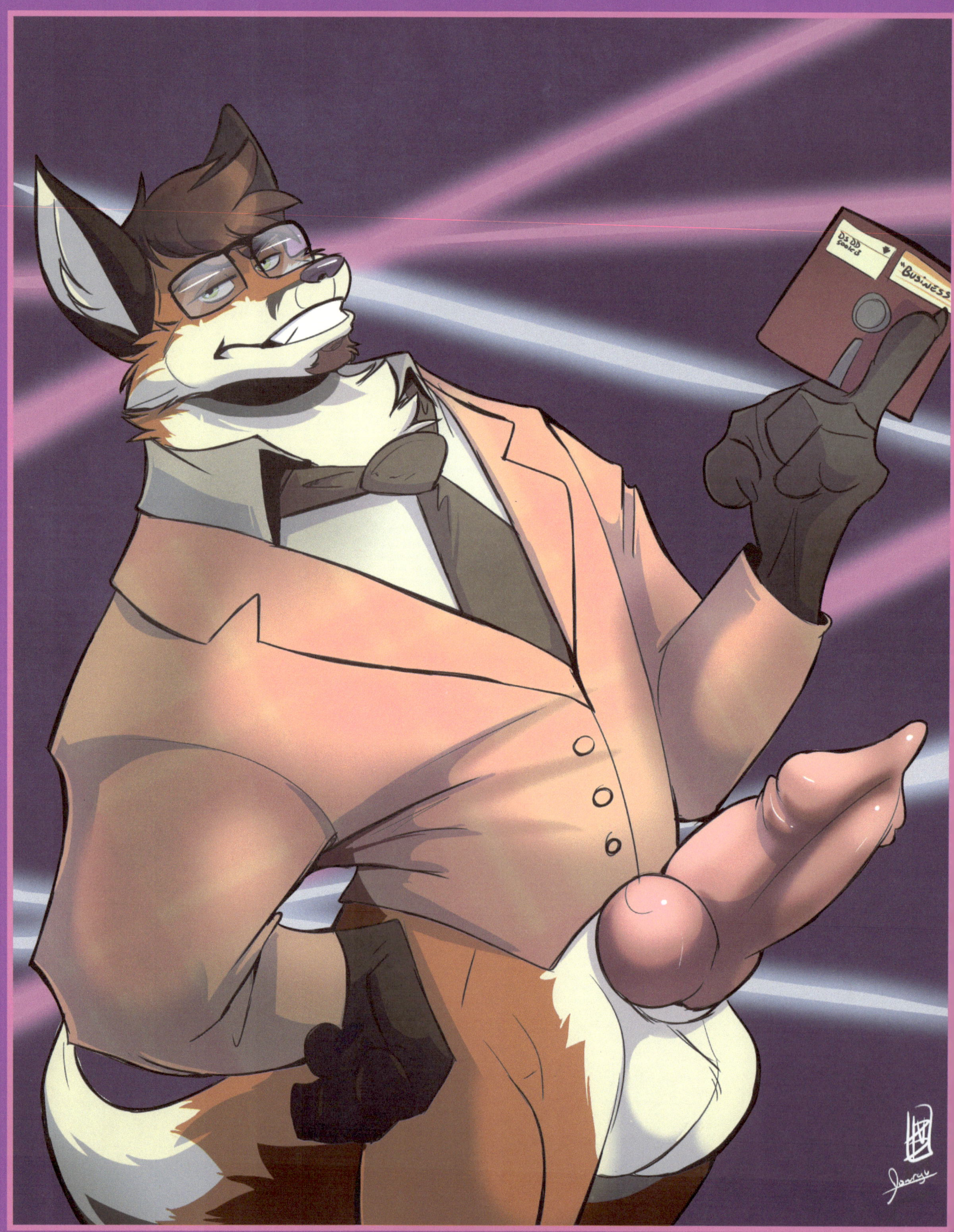
DS DD
"BUSINESS

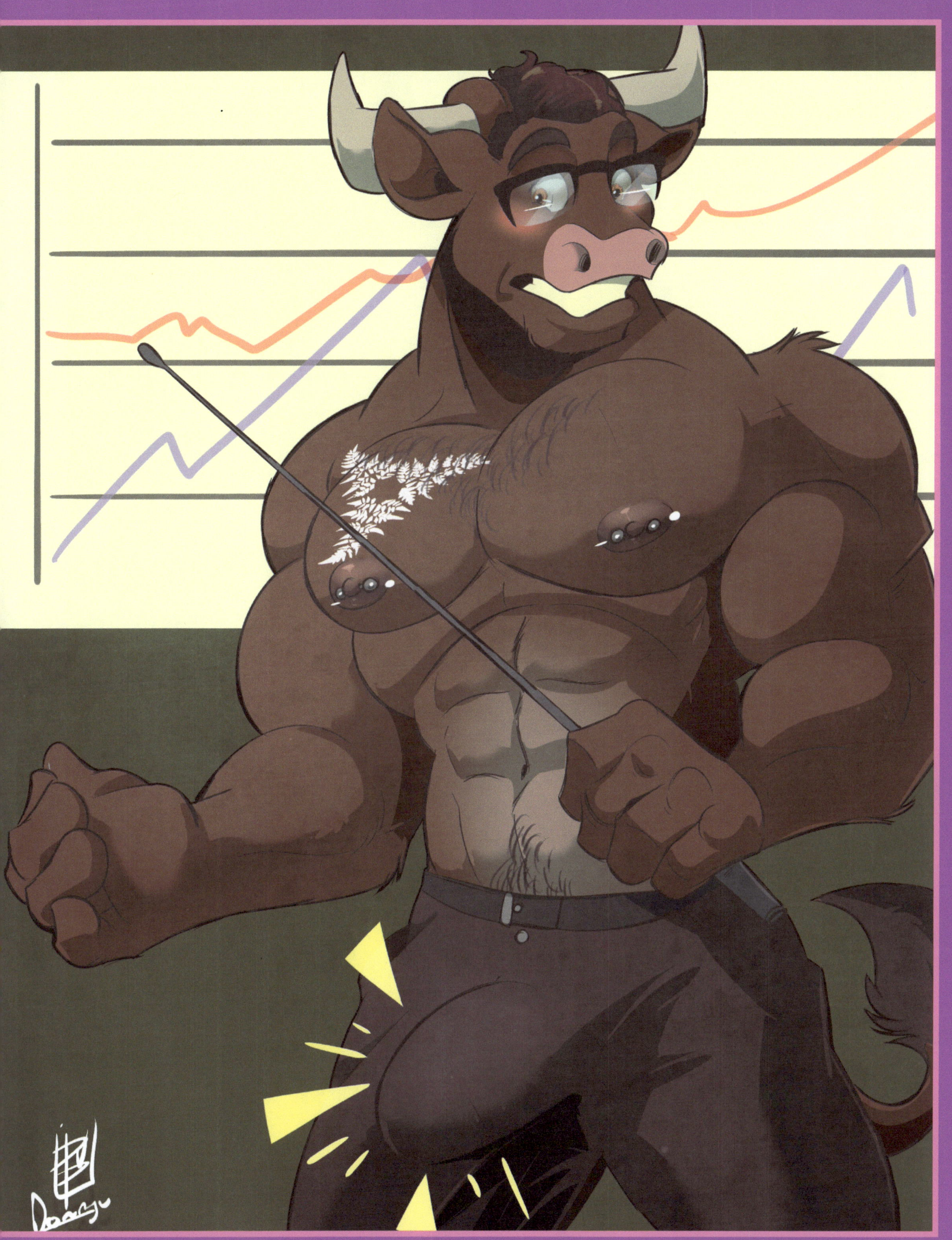

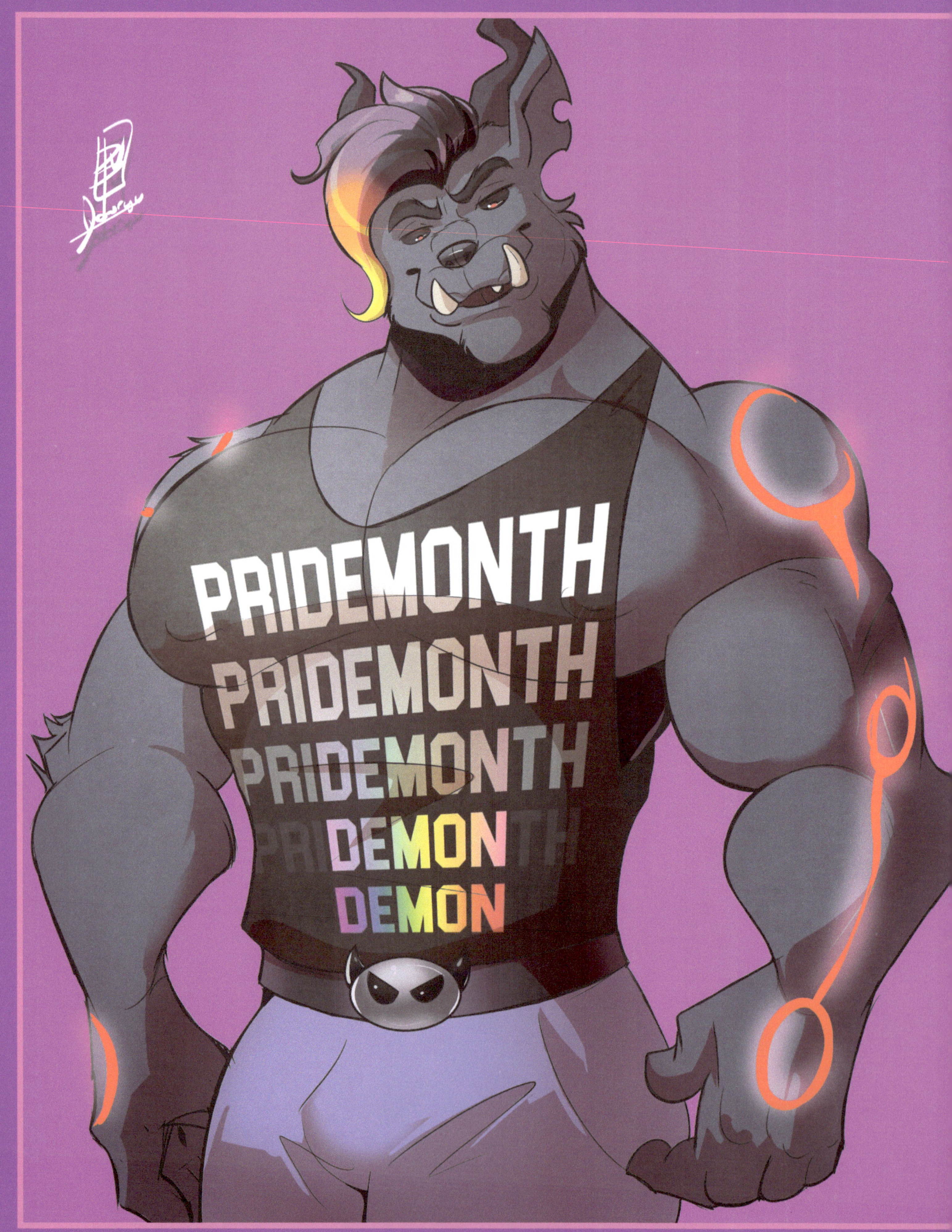
PRIDEMONTH
PRIDEMONTH
PRIDEMONTH
DEMON
DEMON

~~TITTIES~~ BUSTS

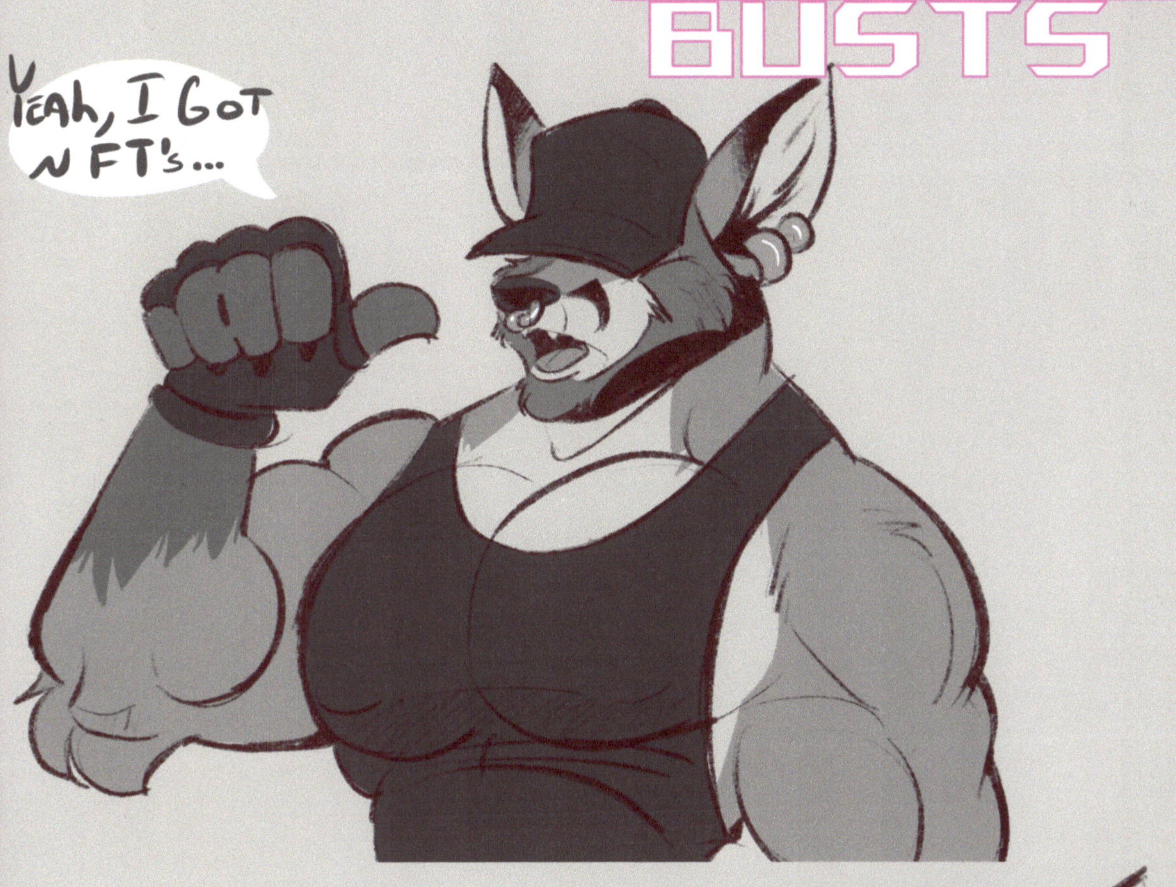

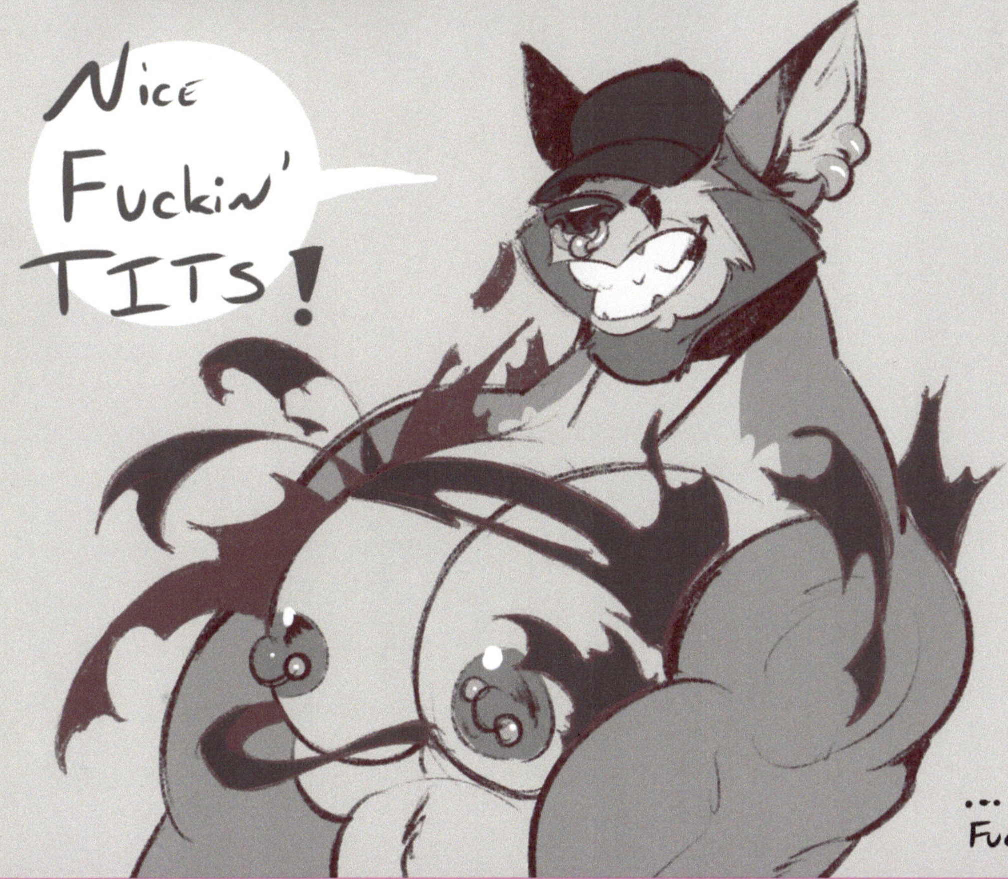

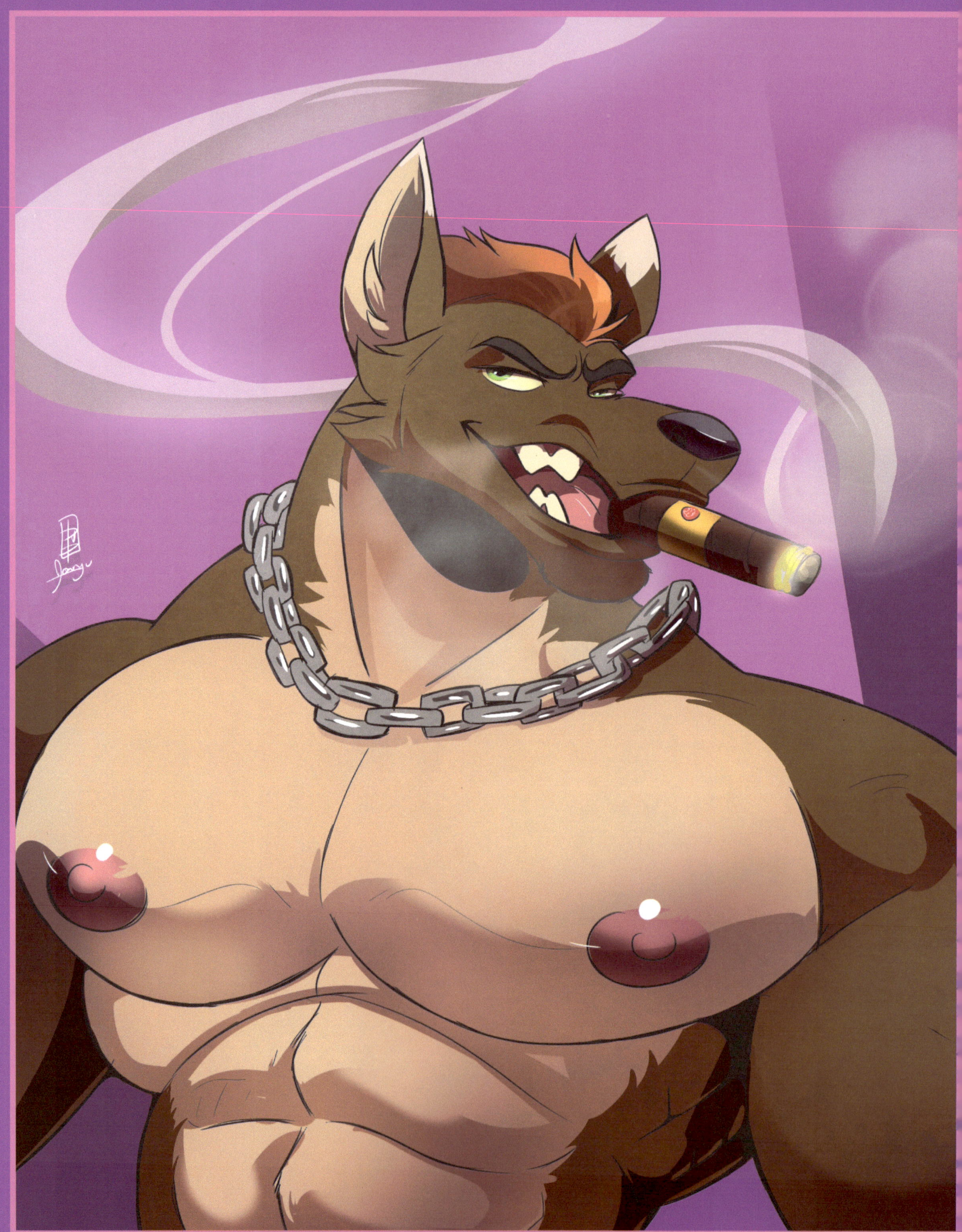

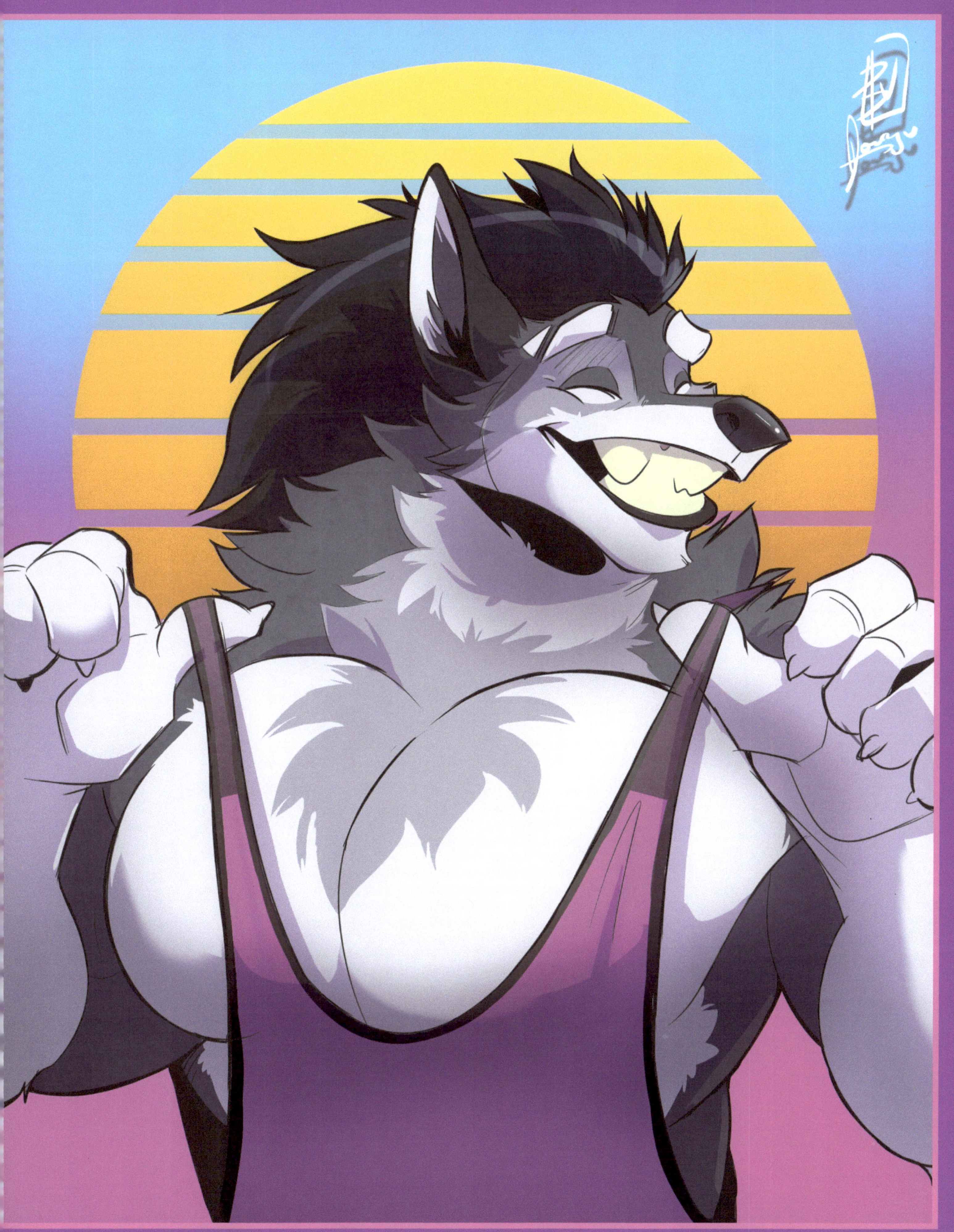

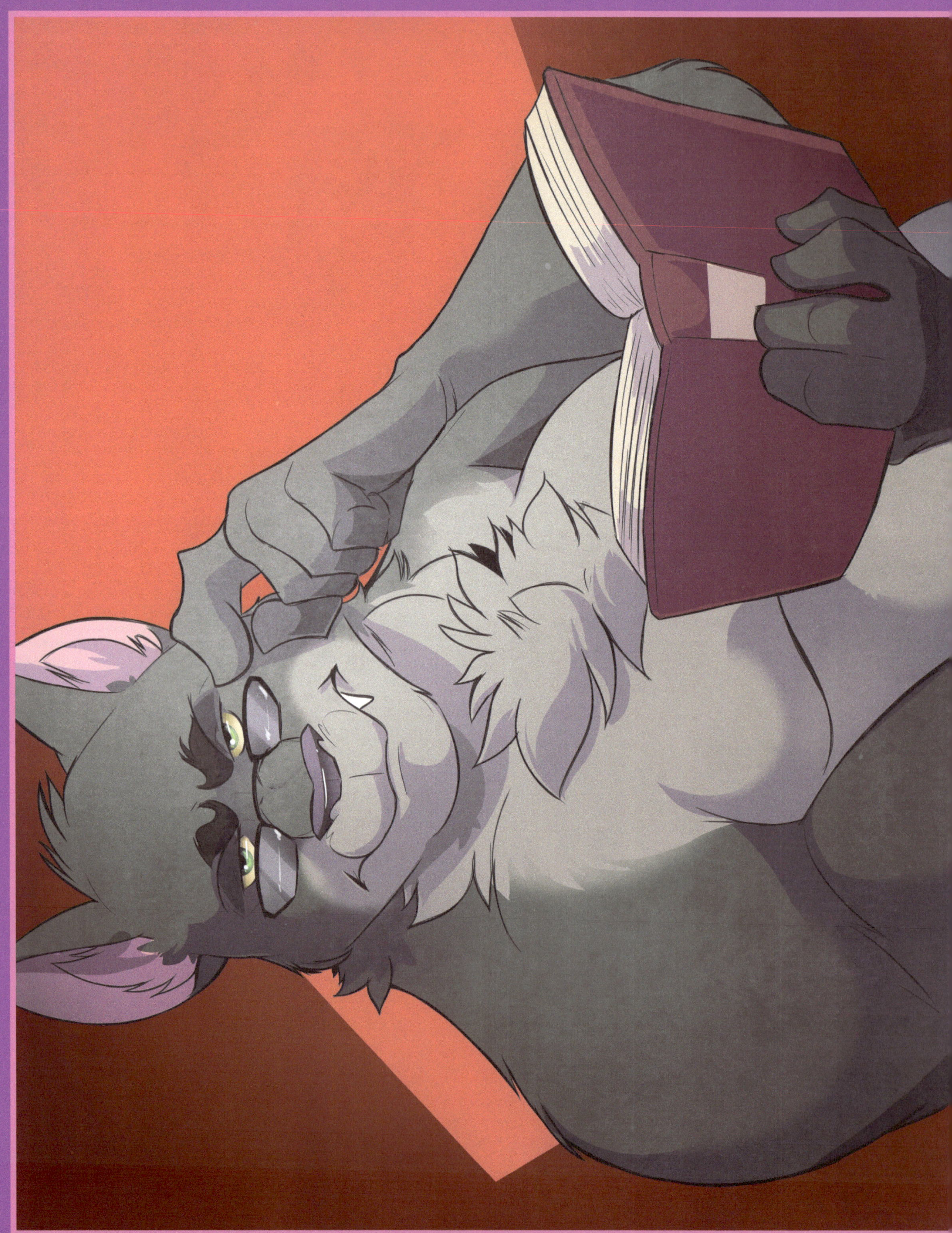

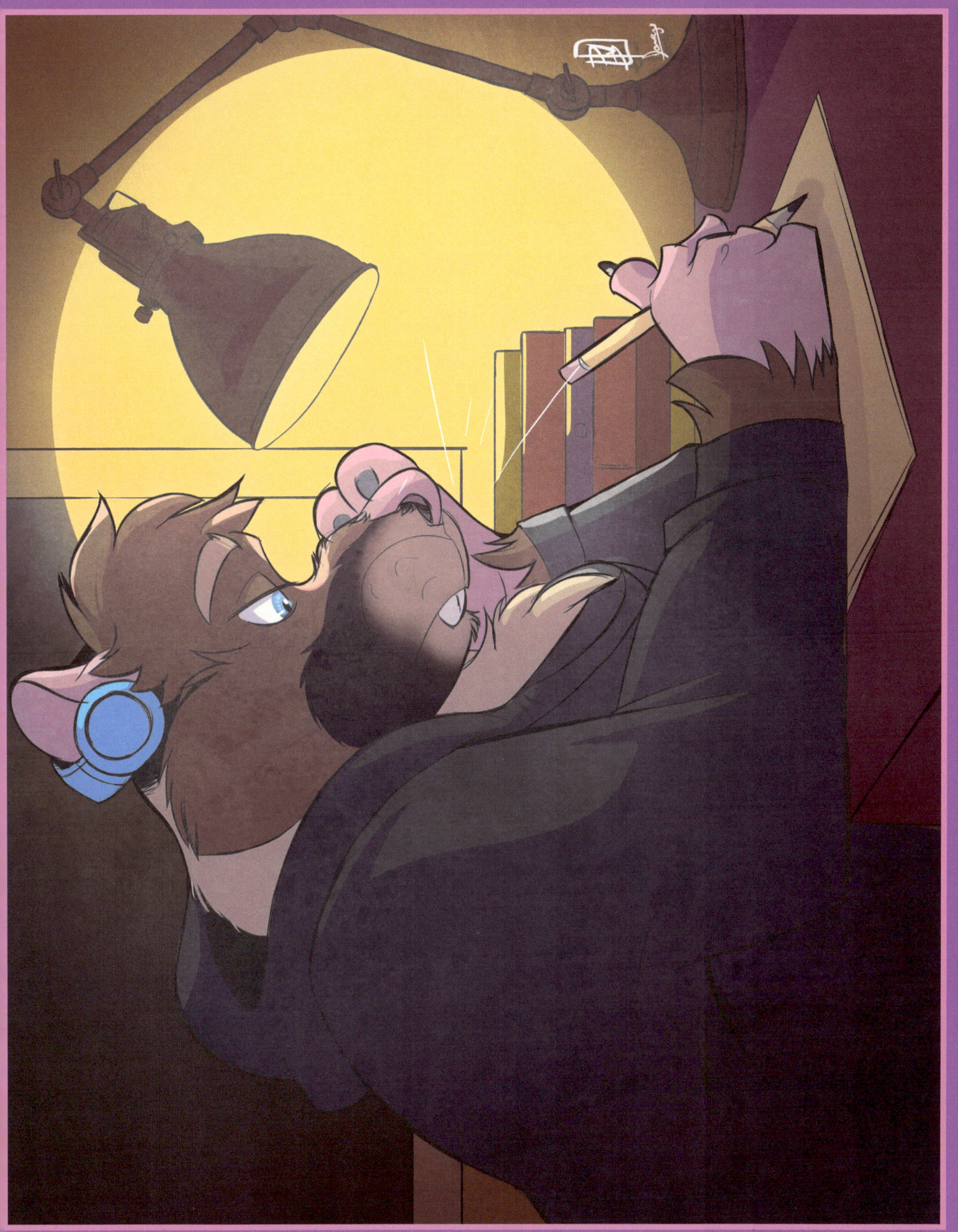

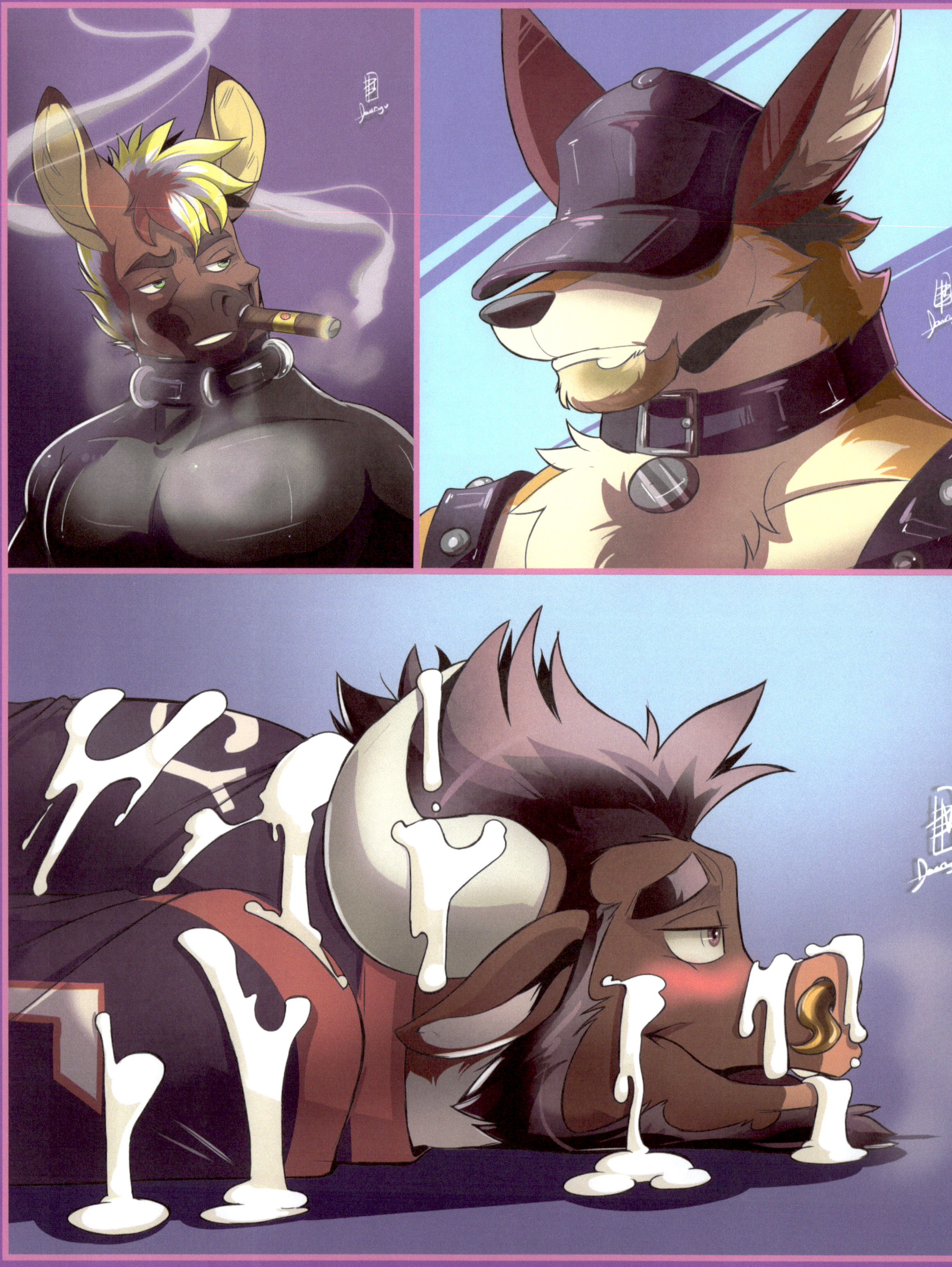

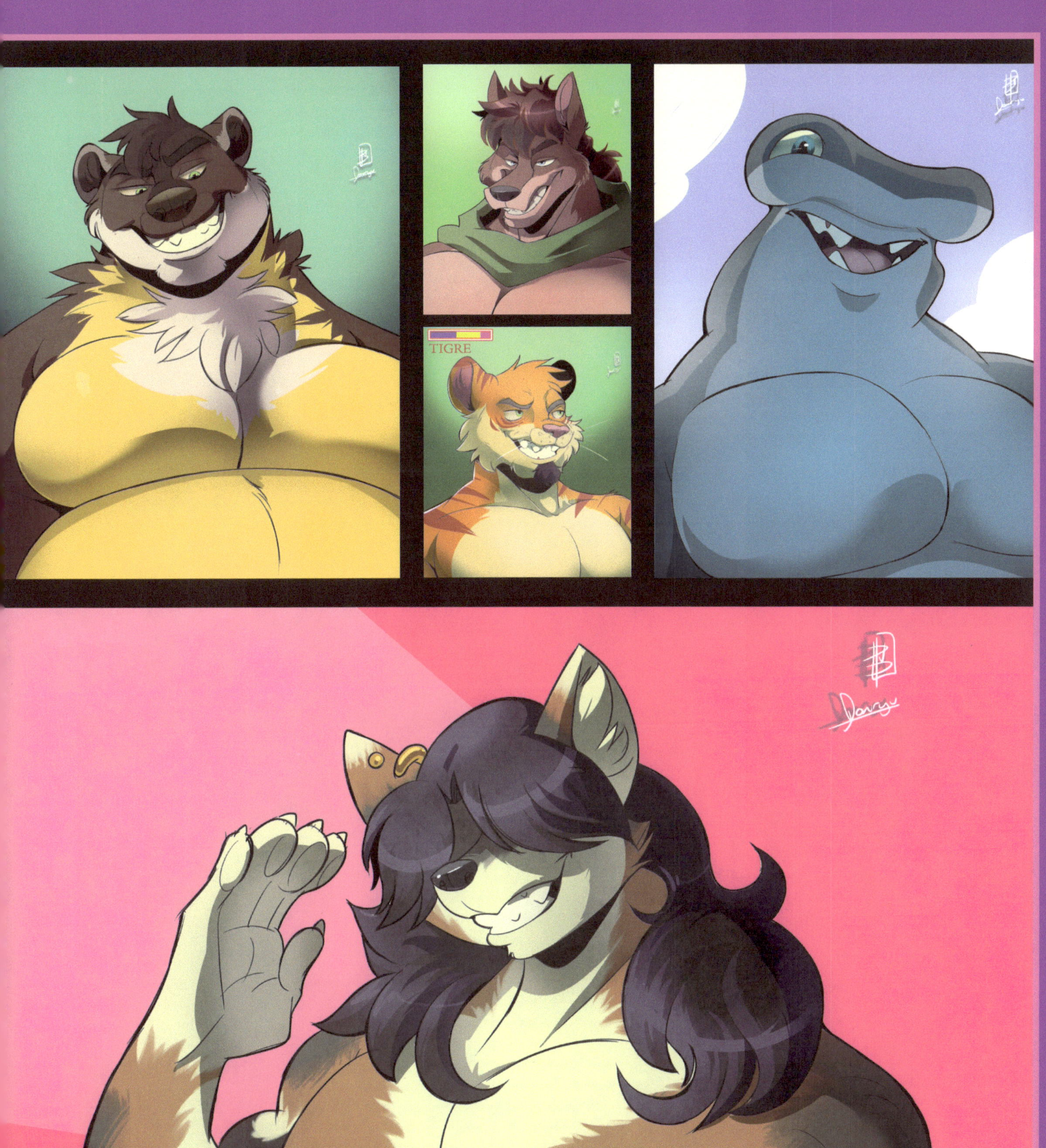
TIGRE

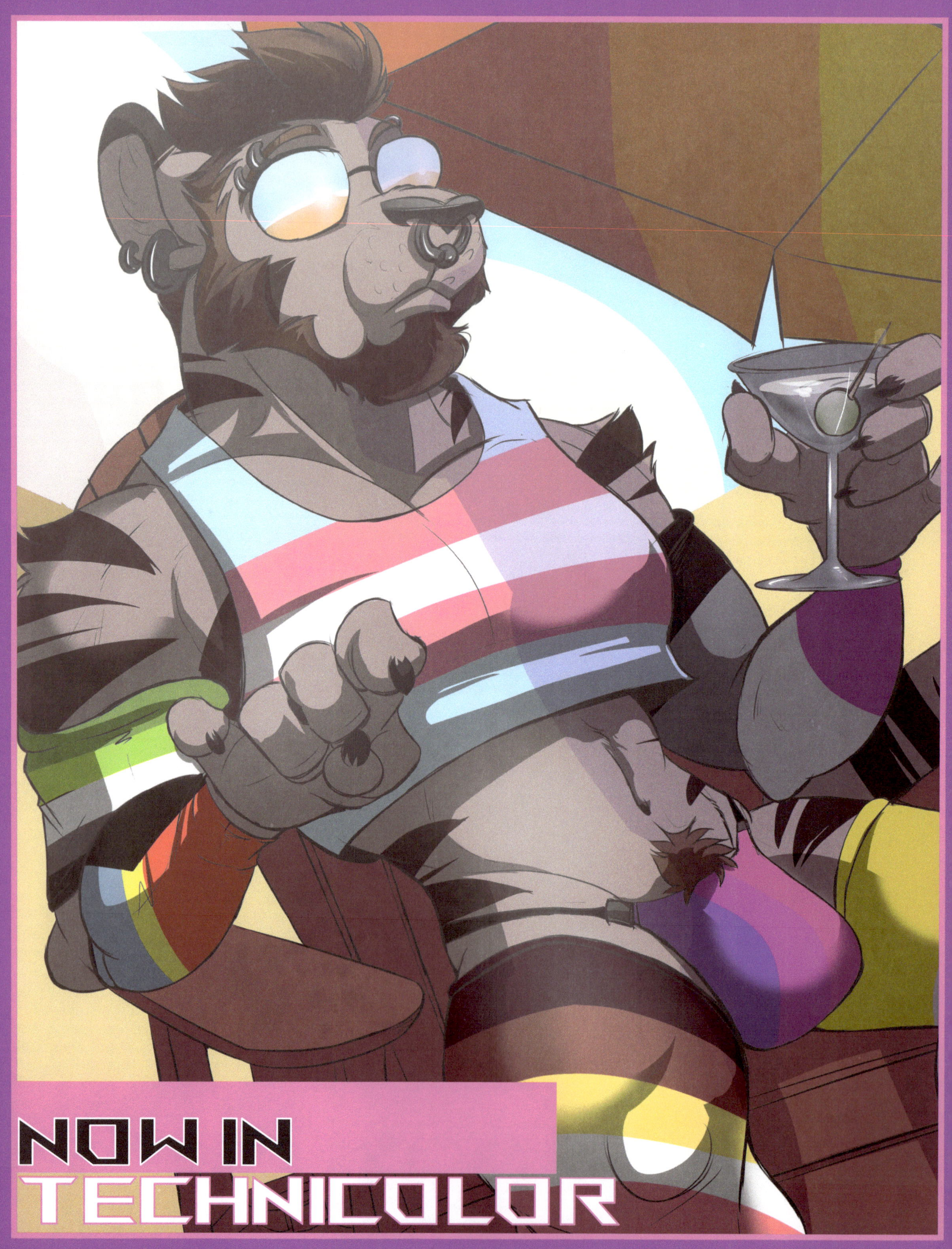
NOW IN
TECHNICOLOR

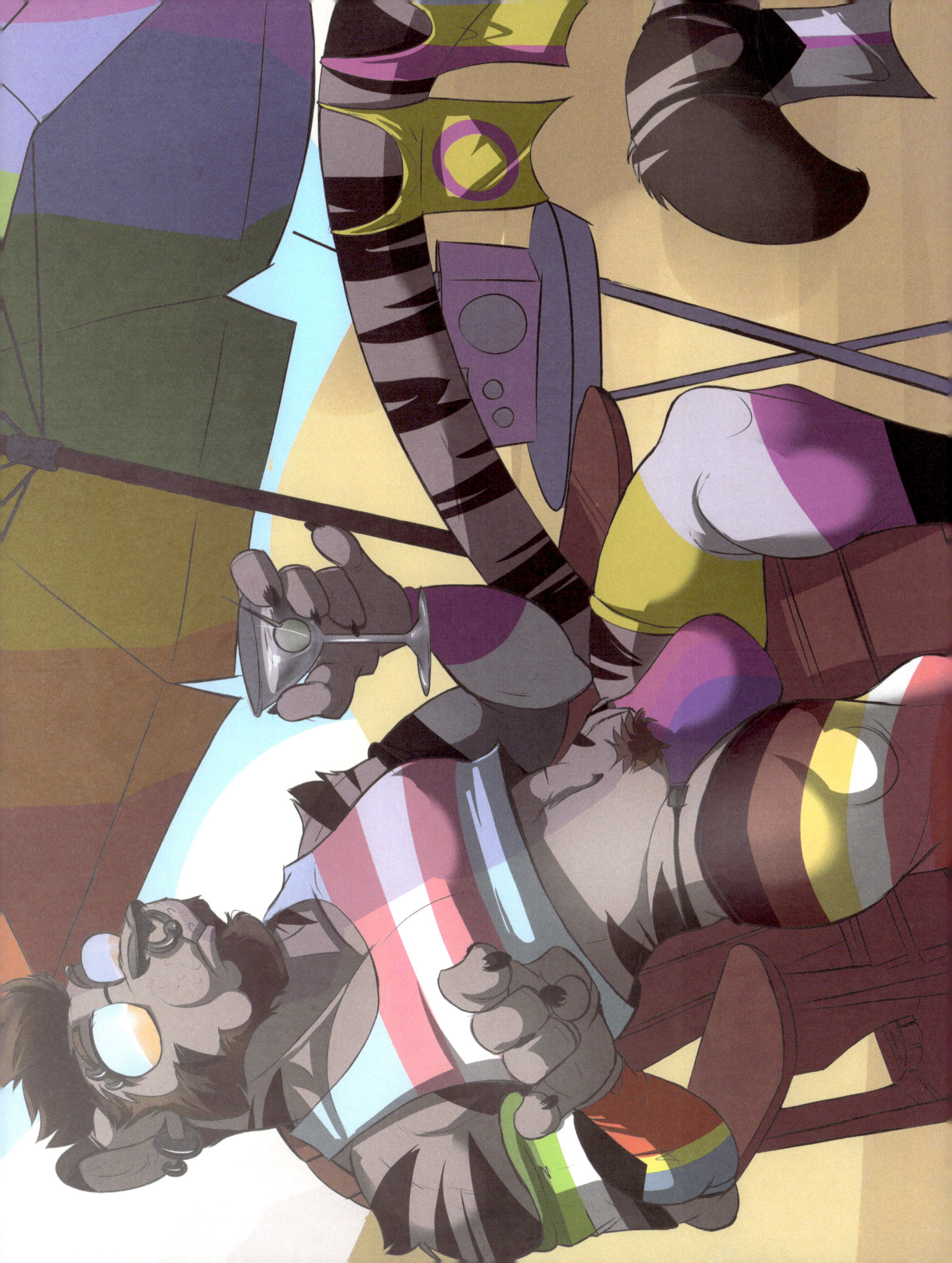

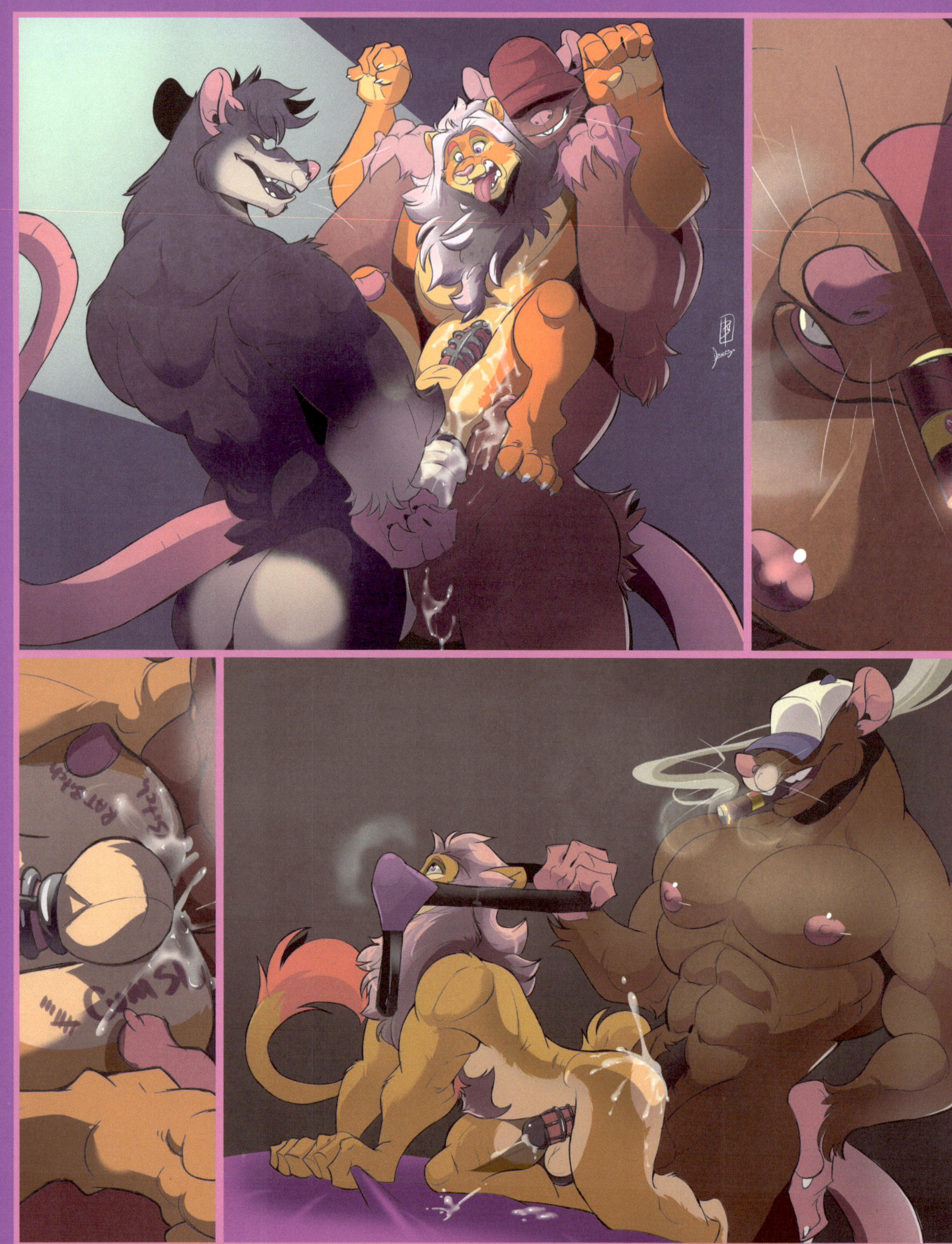
Rat Bitch
Suck

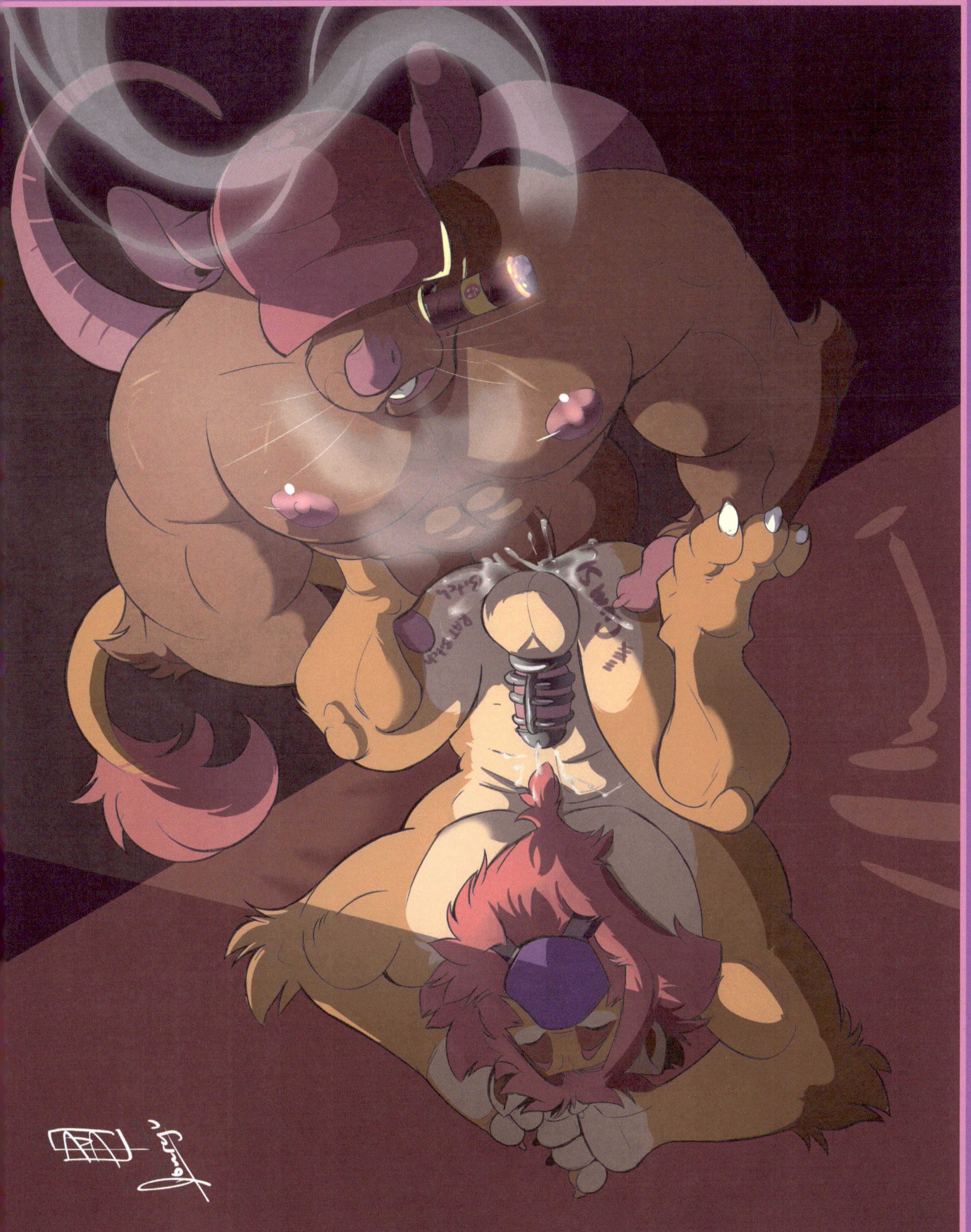

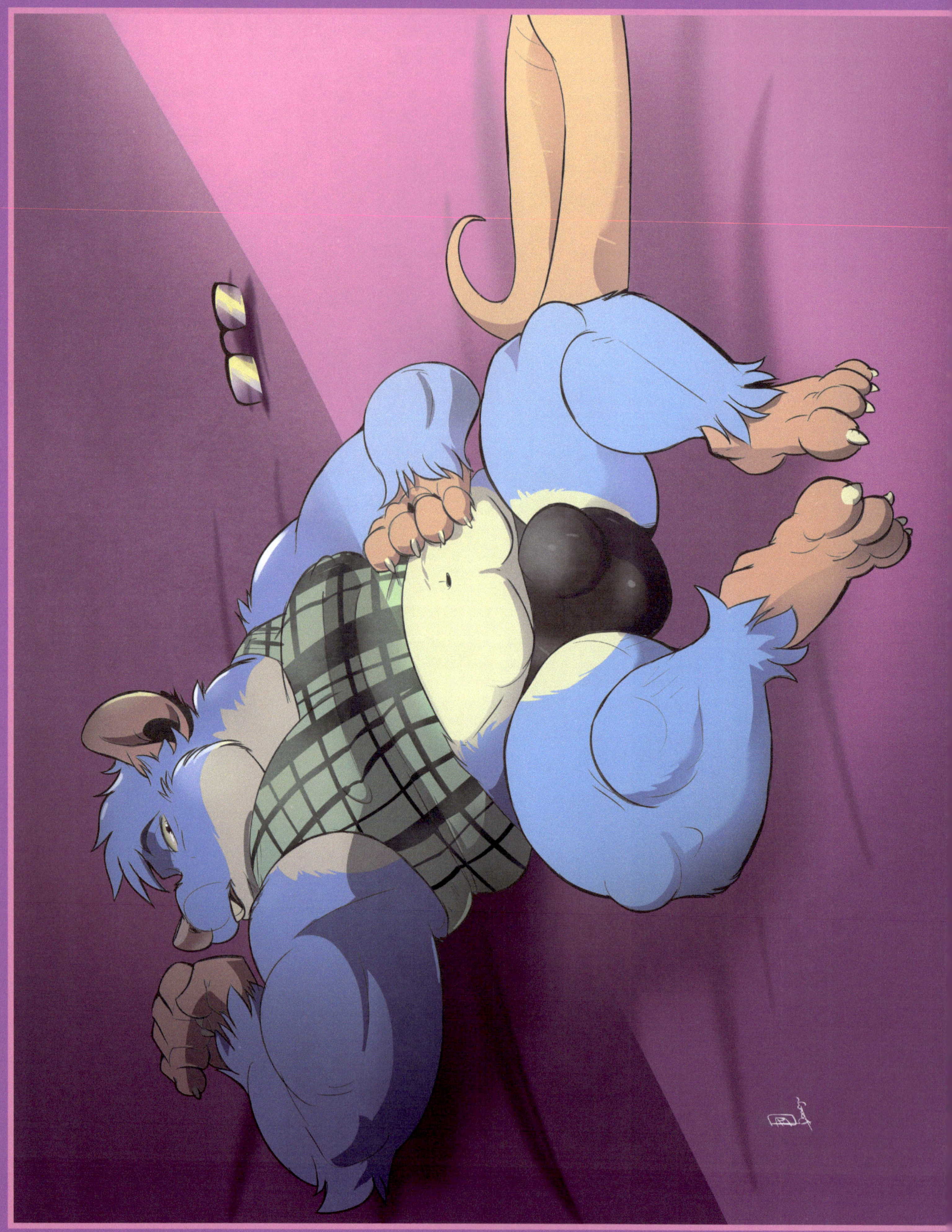

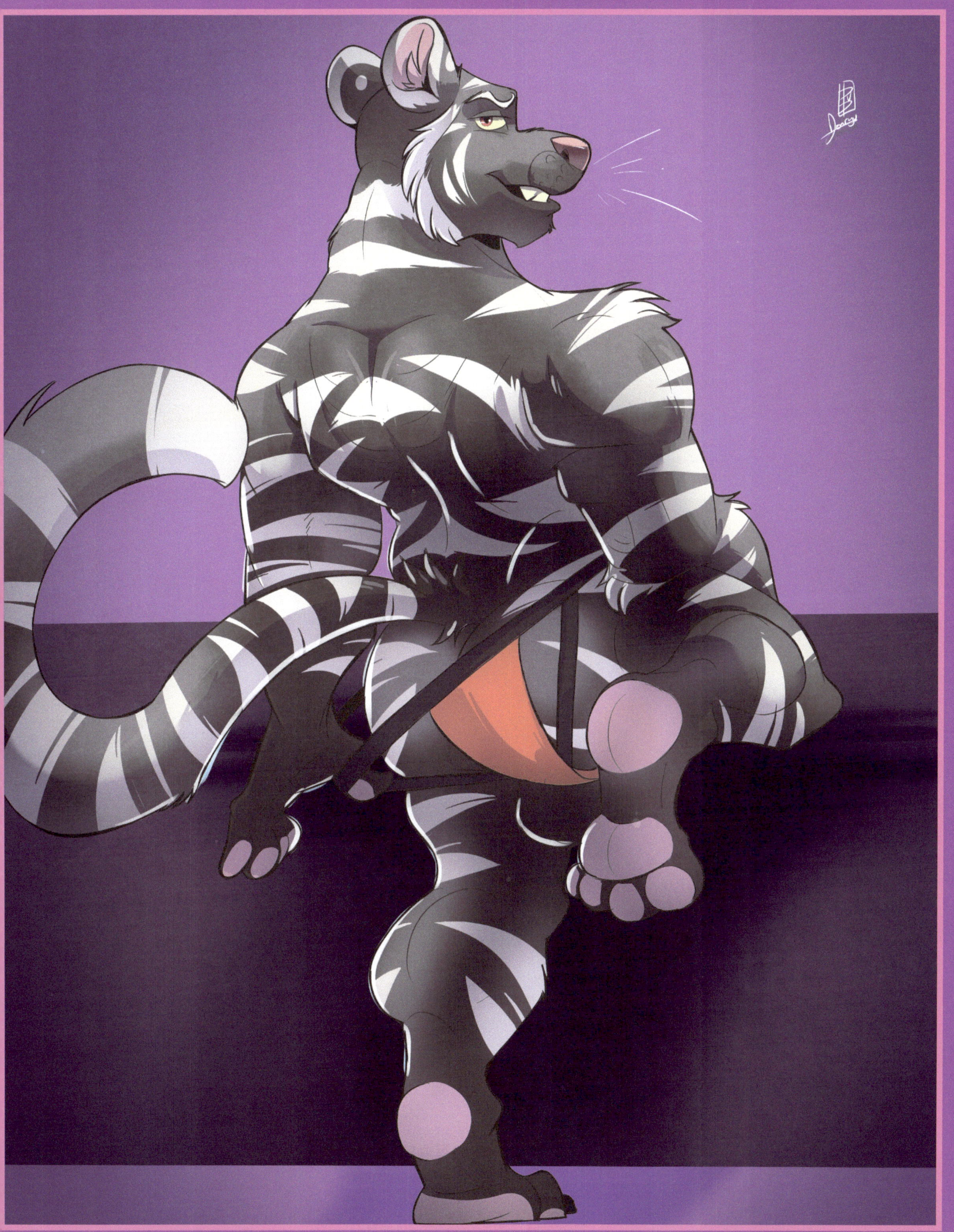

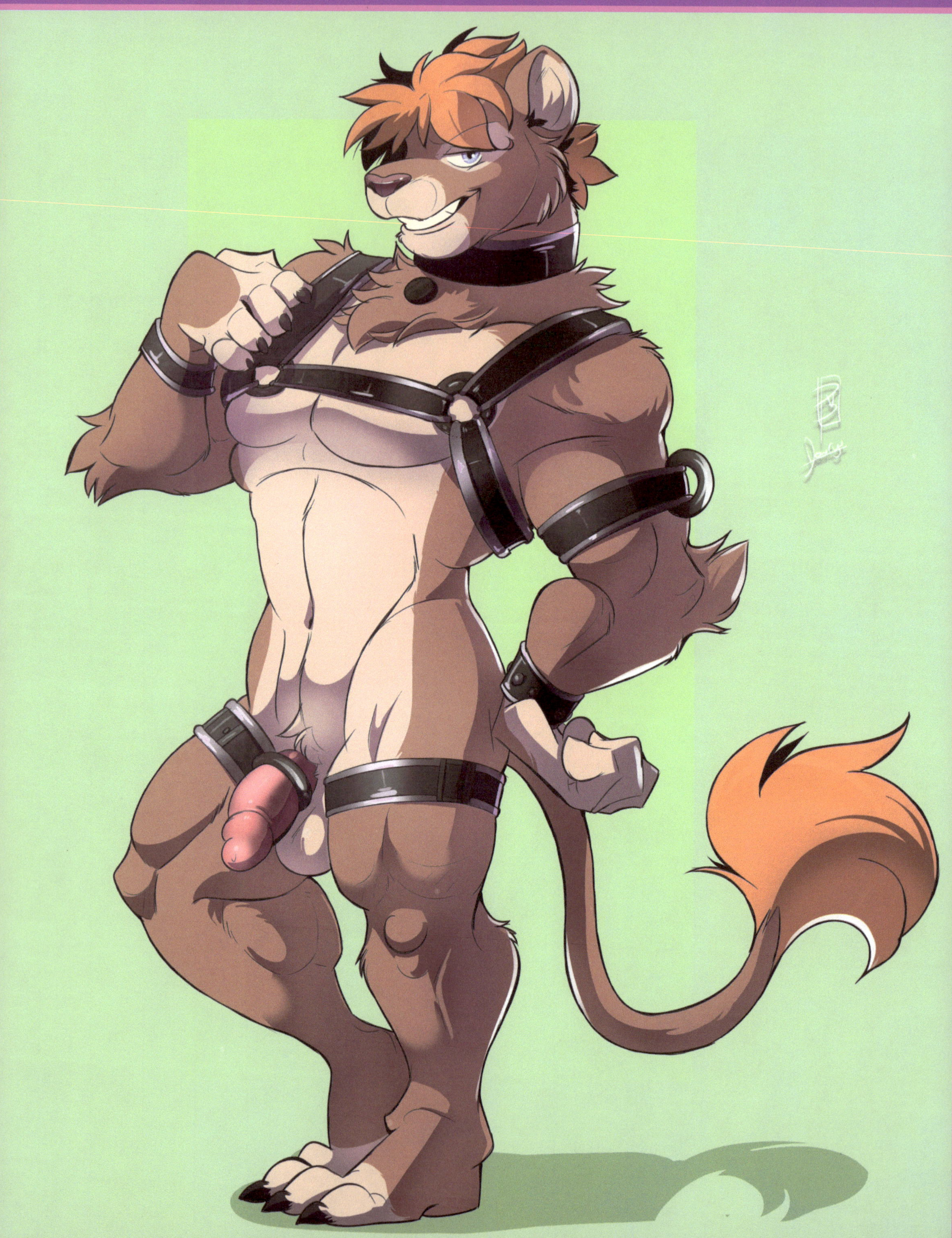

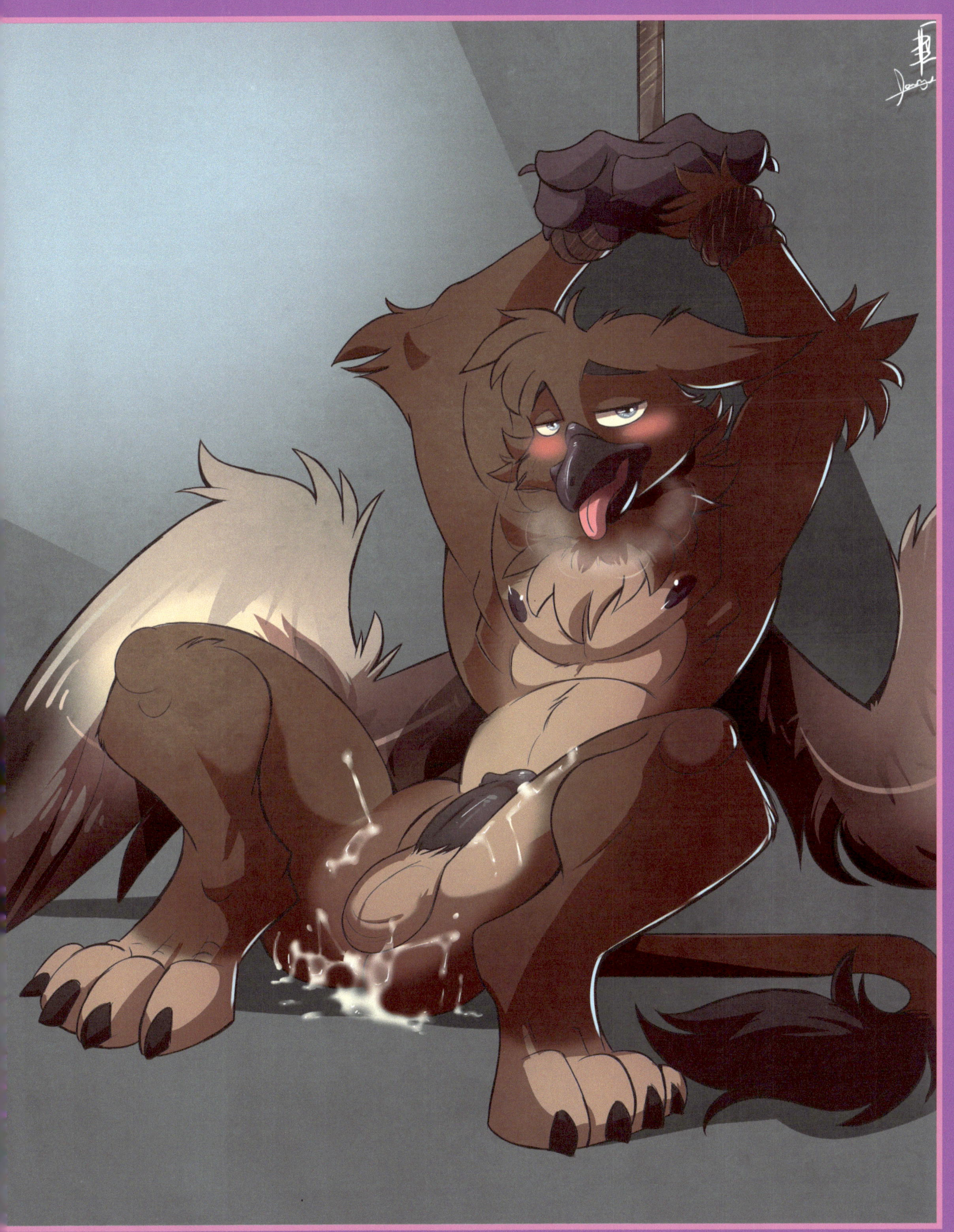

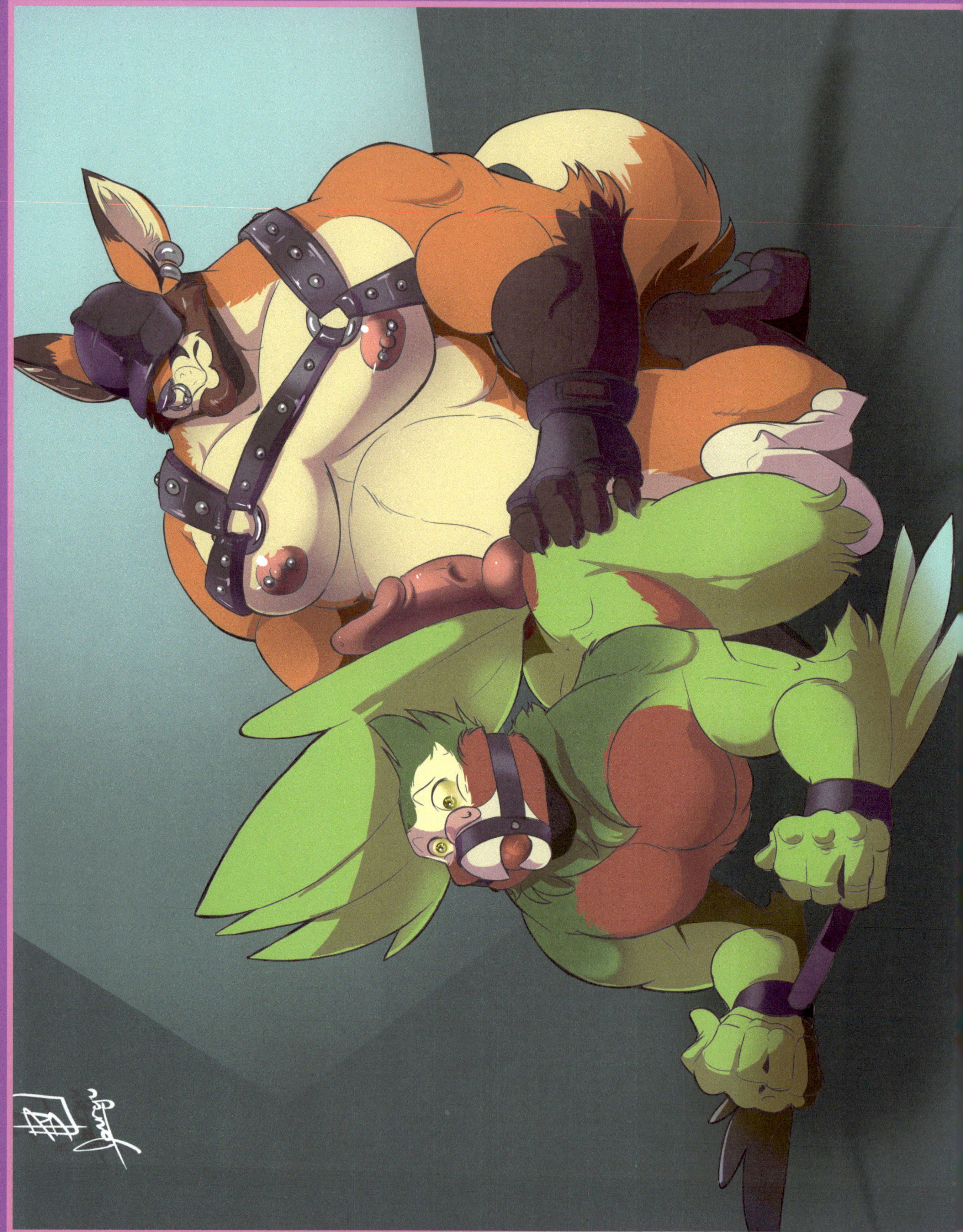

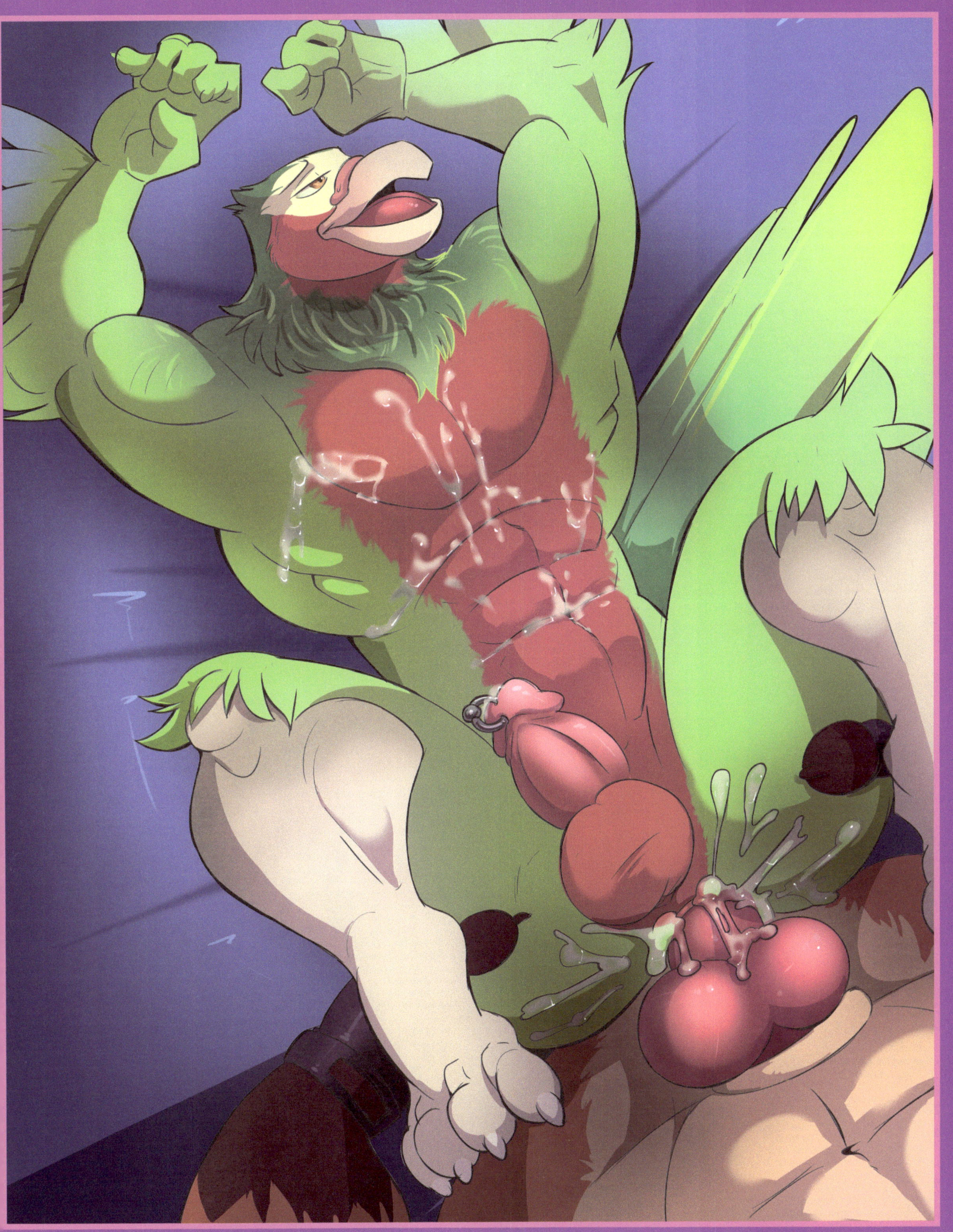

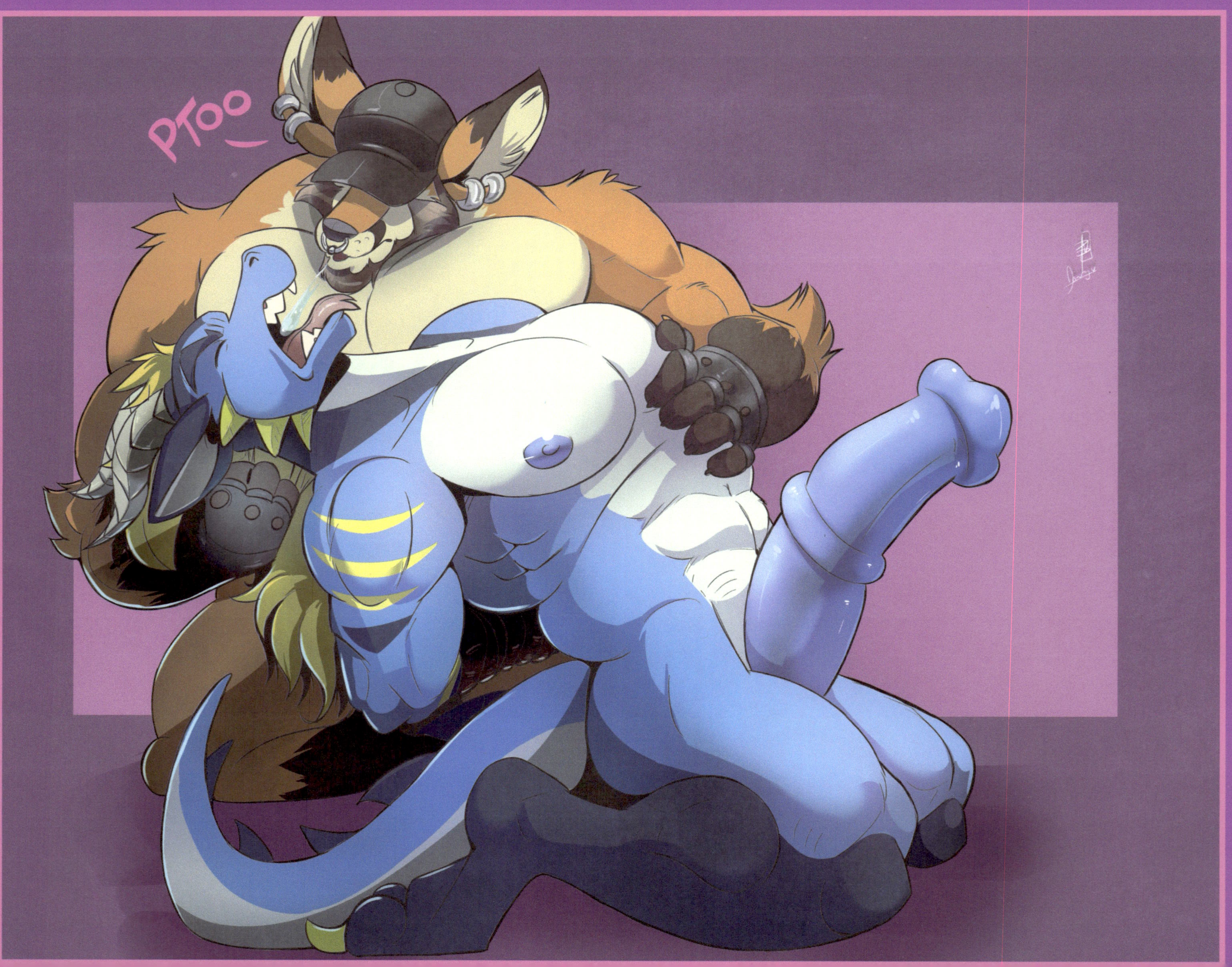
PTOO~

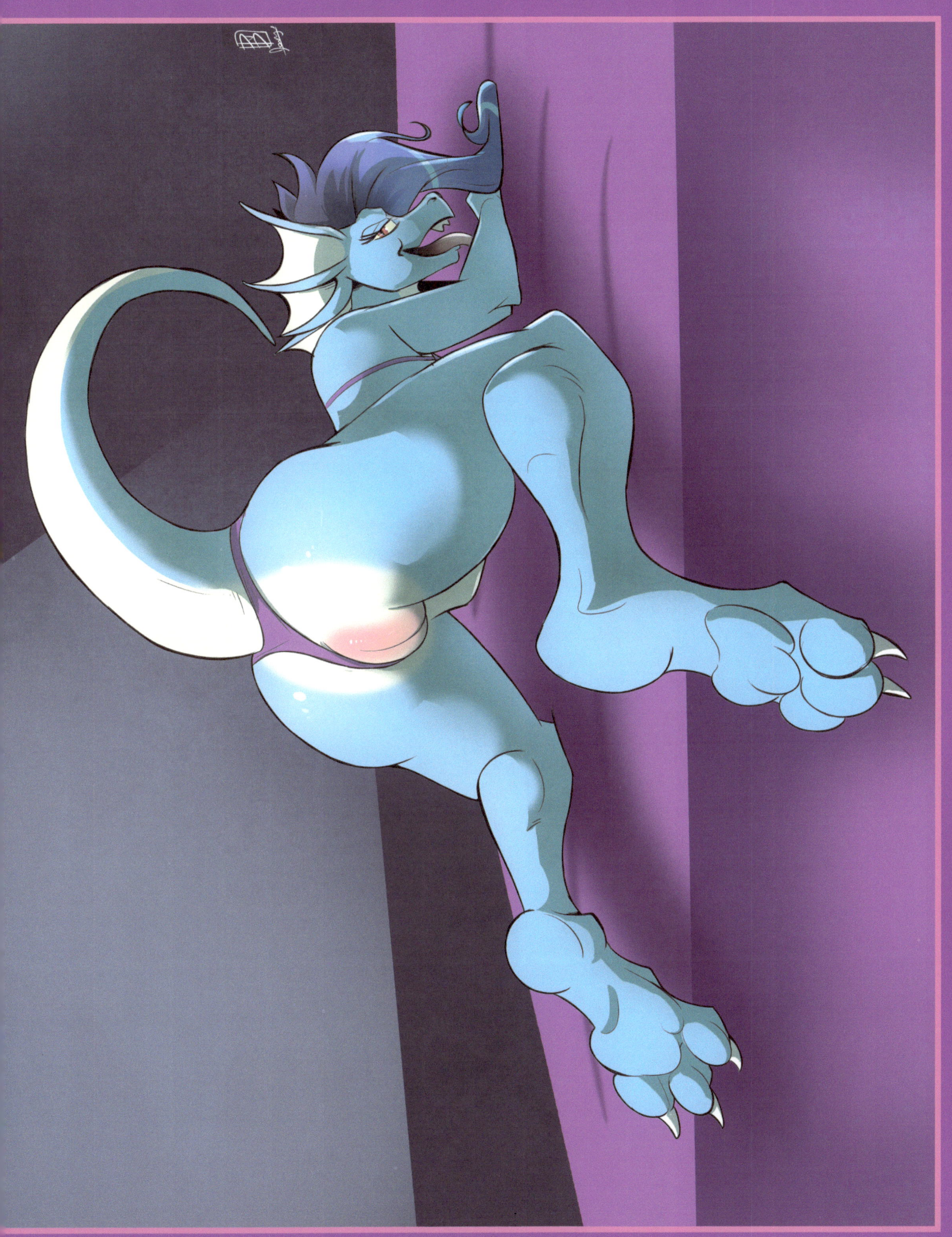

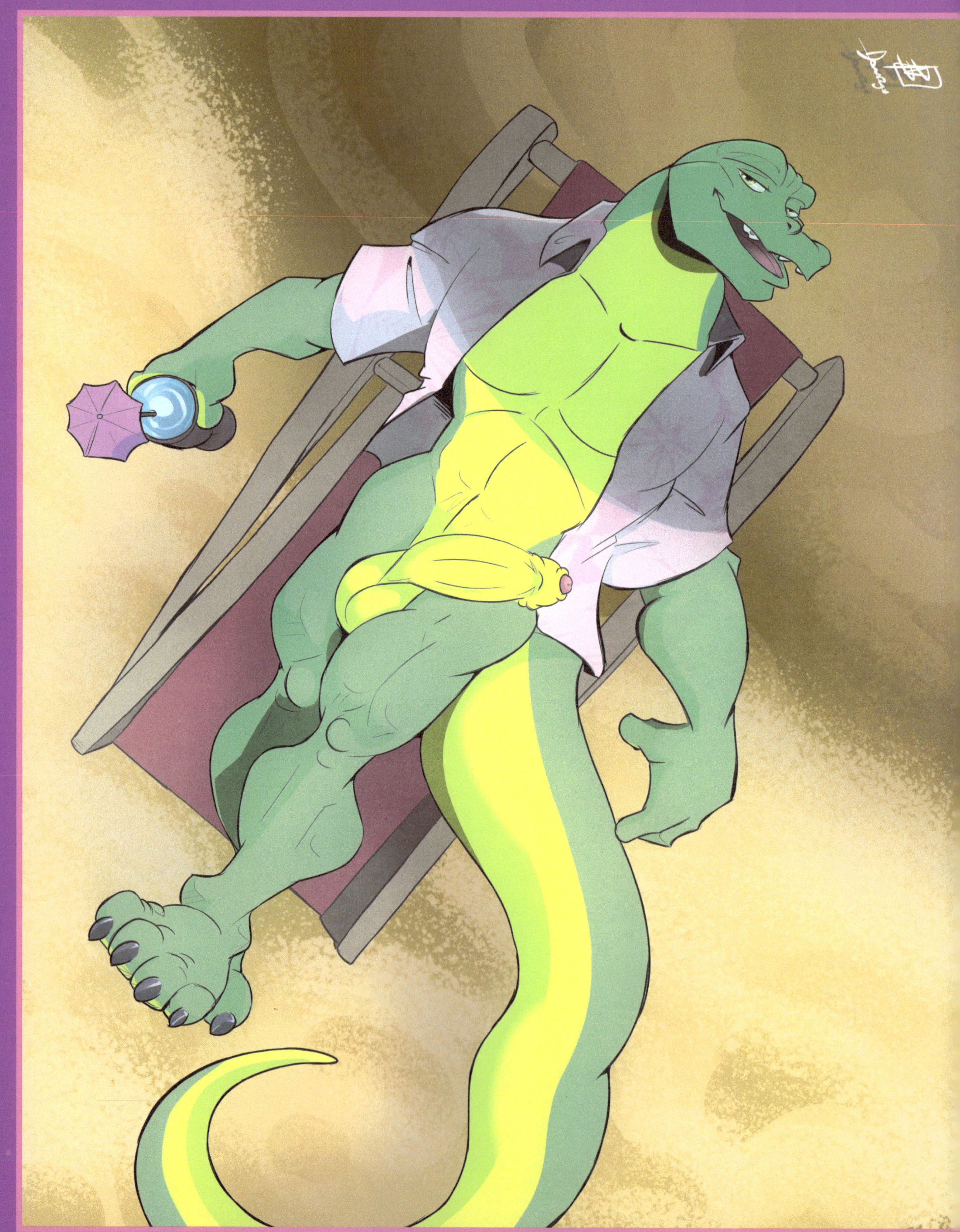

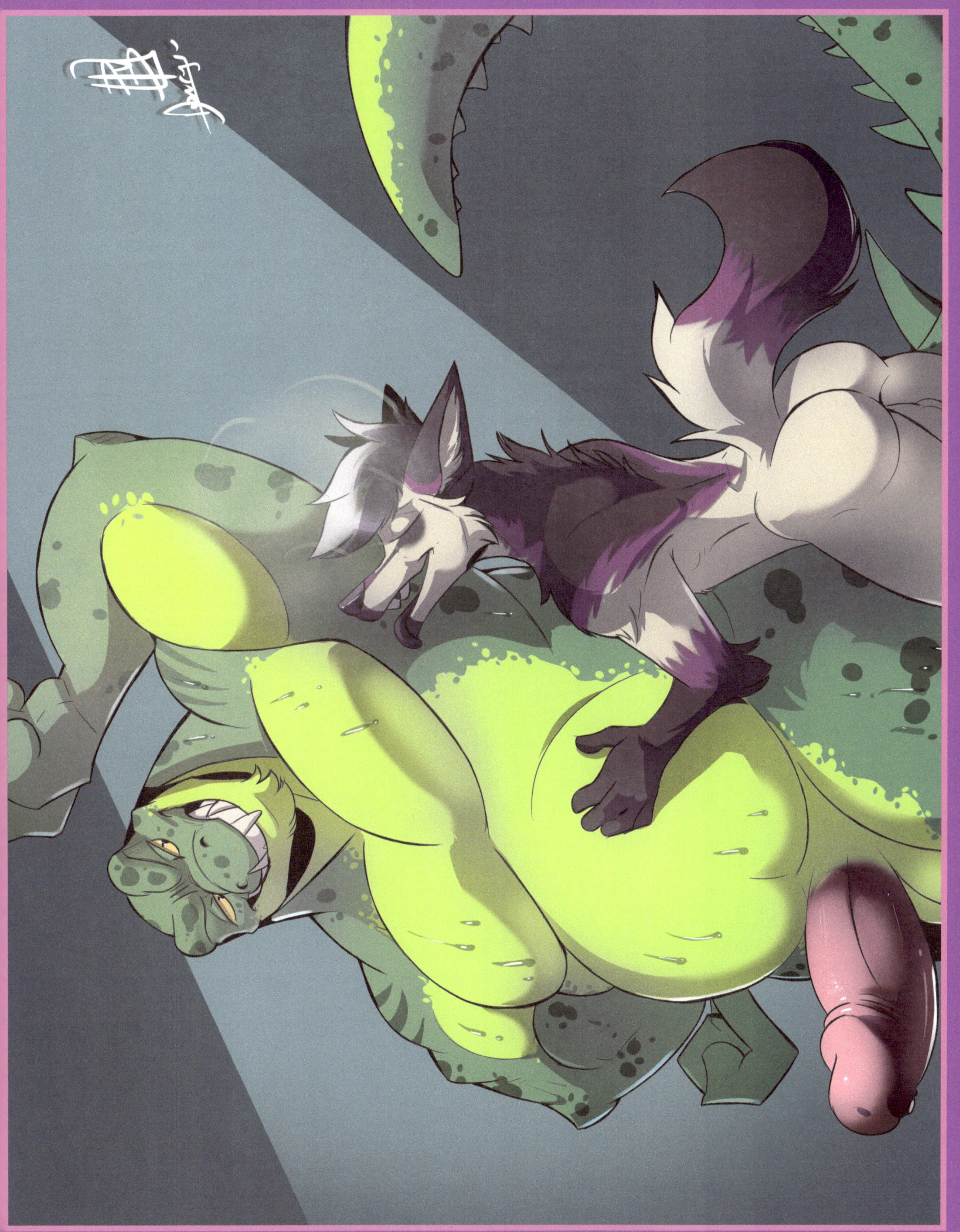

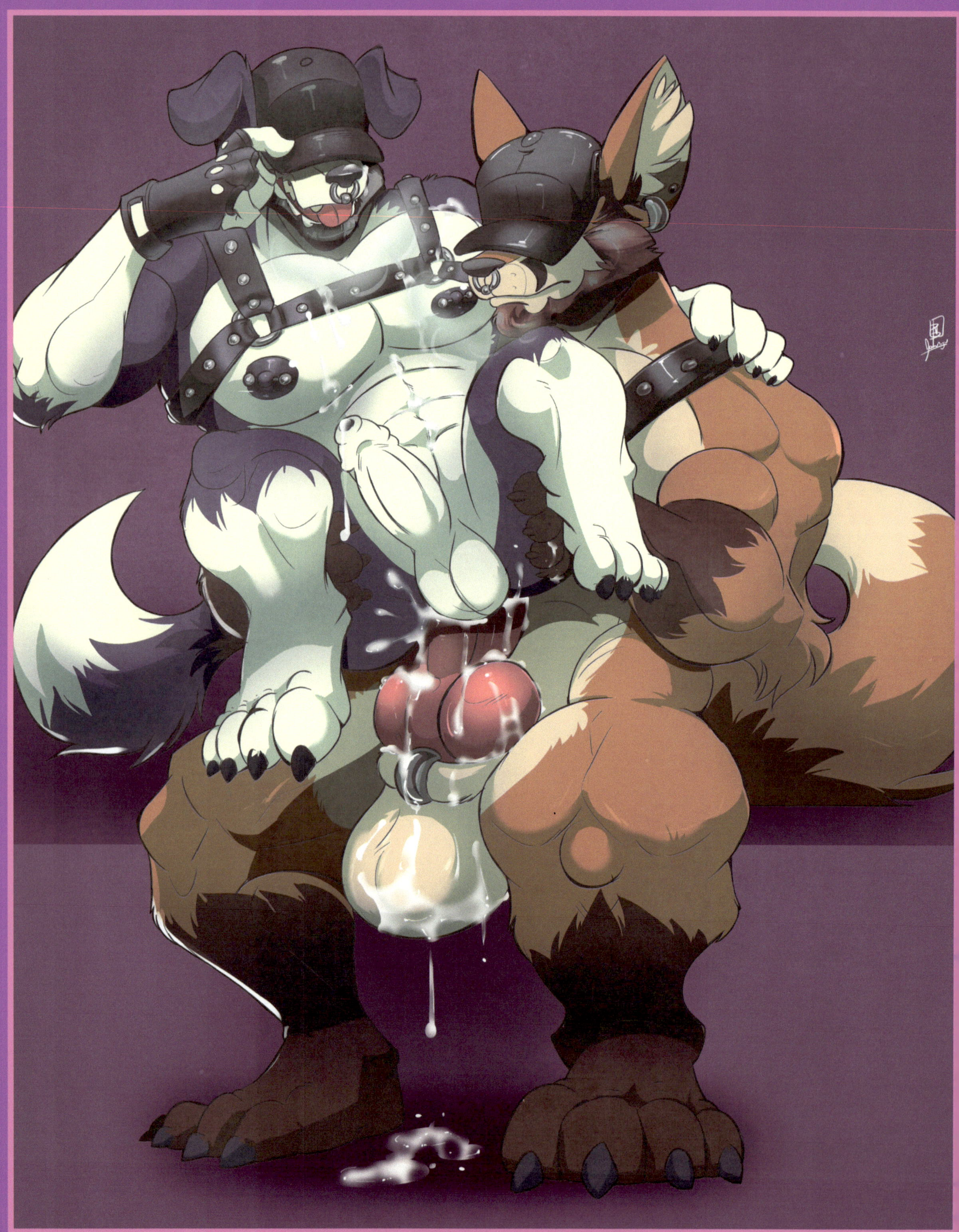

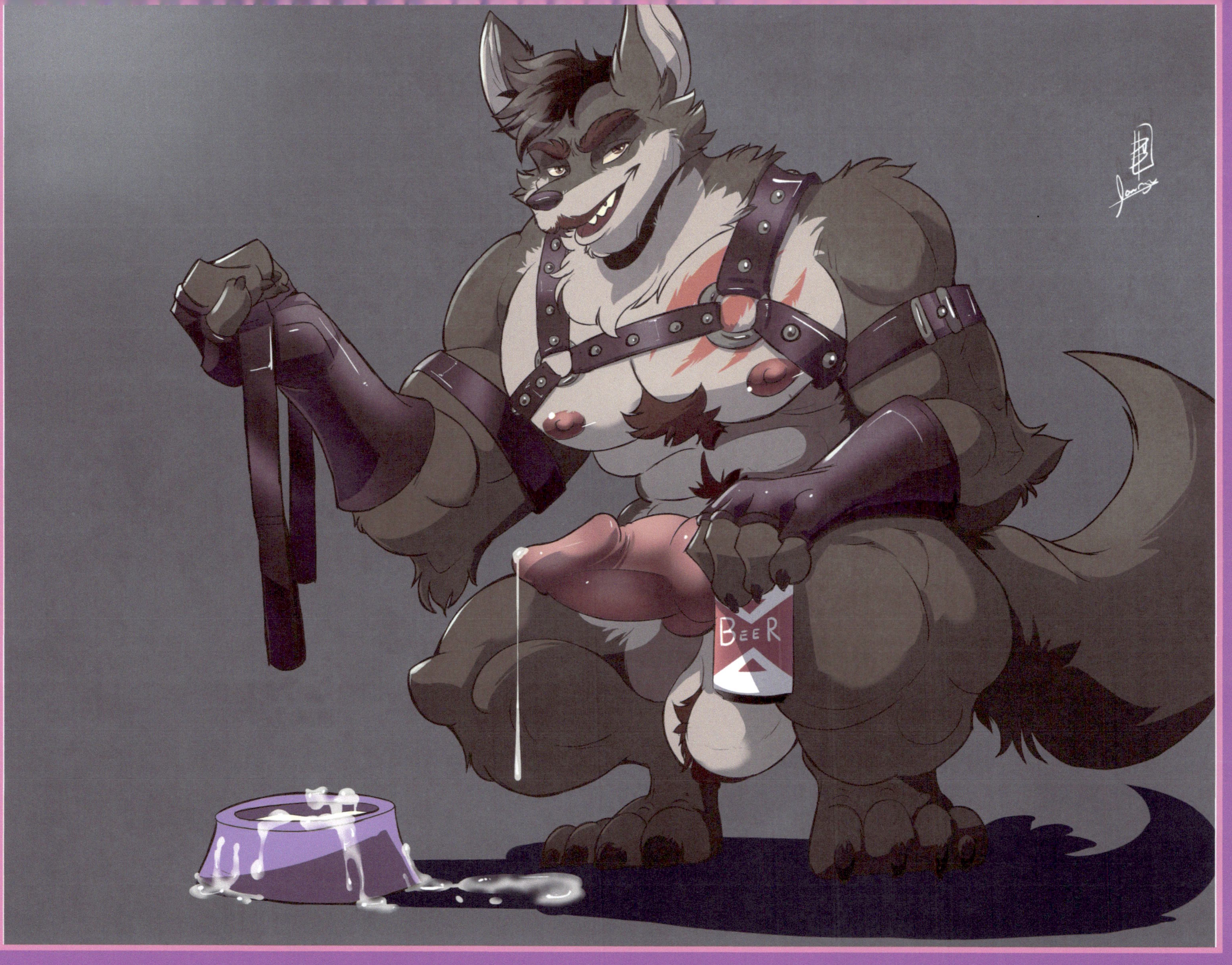
BEER

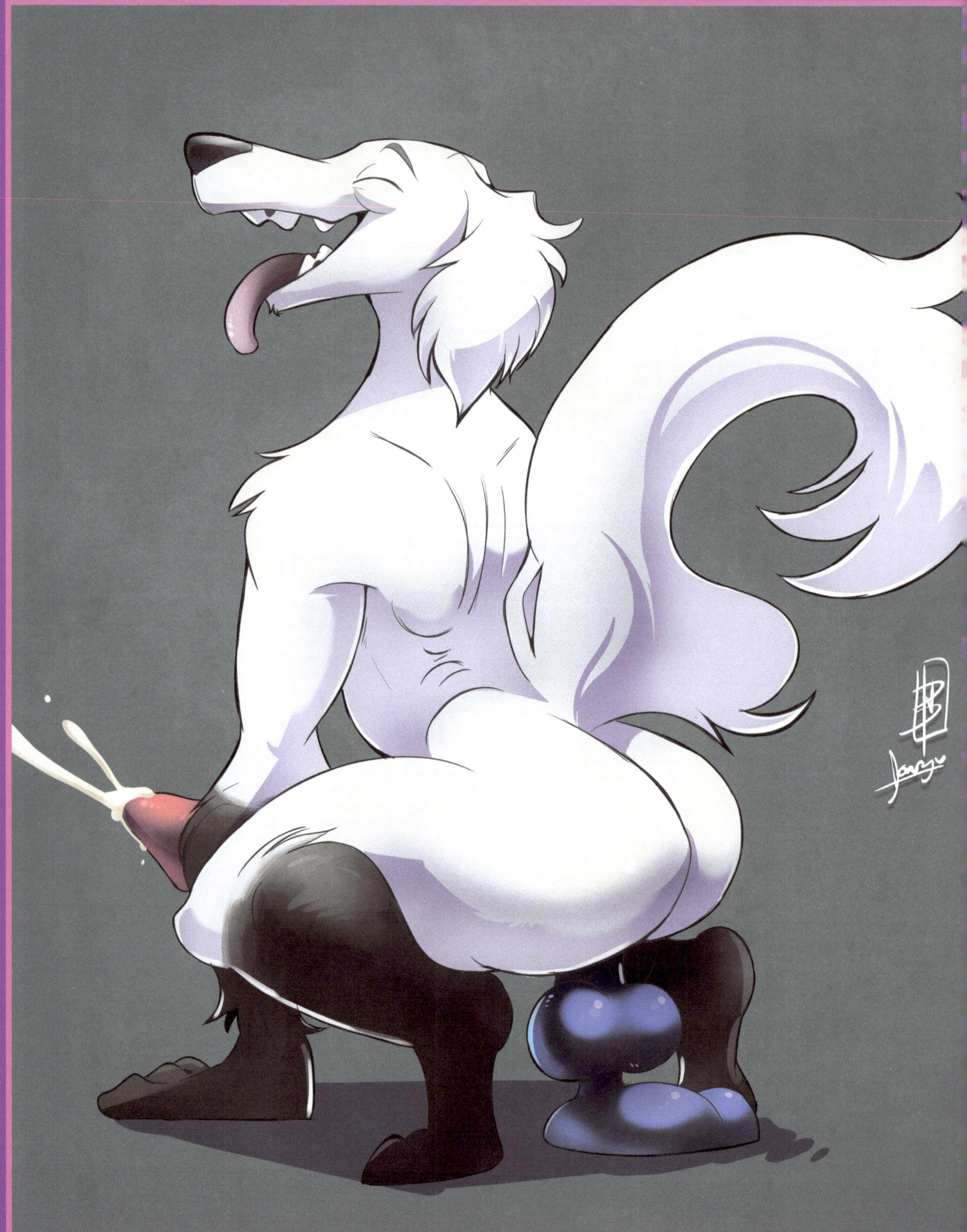

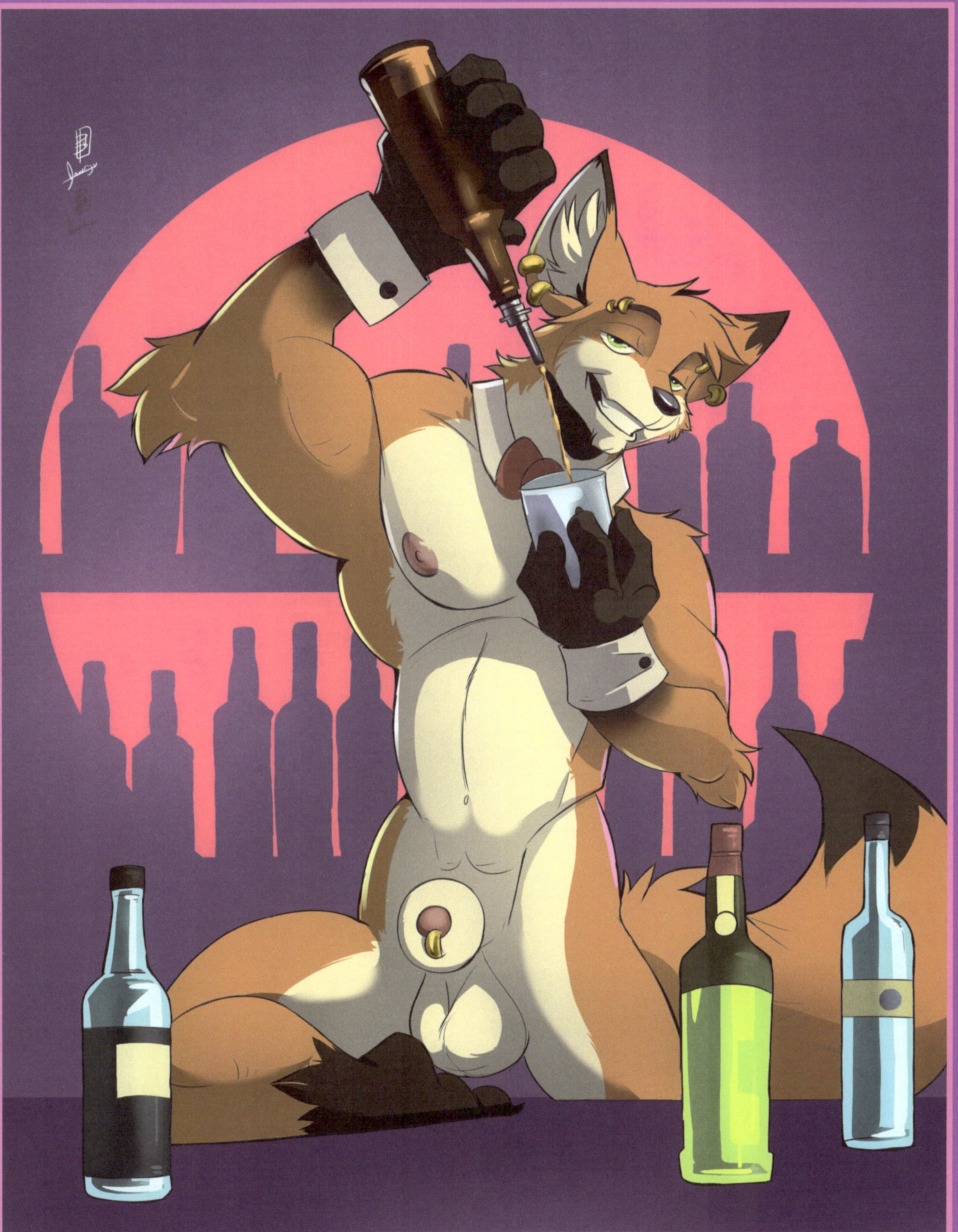

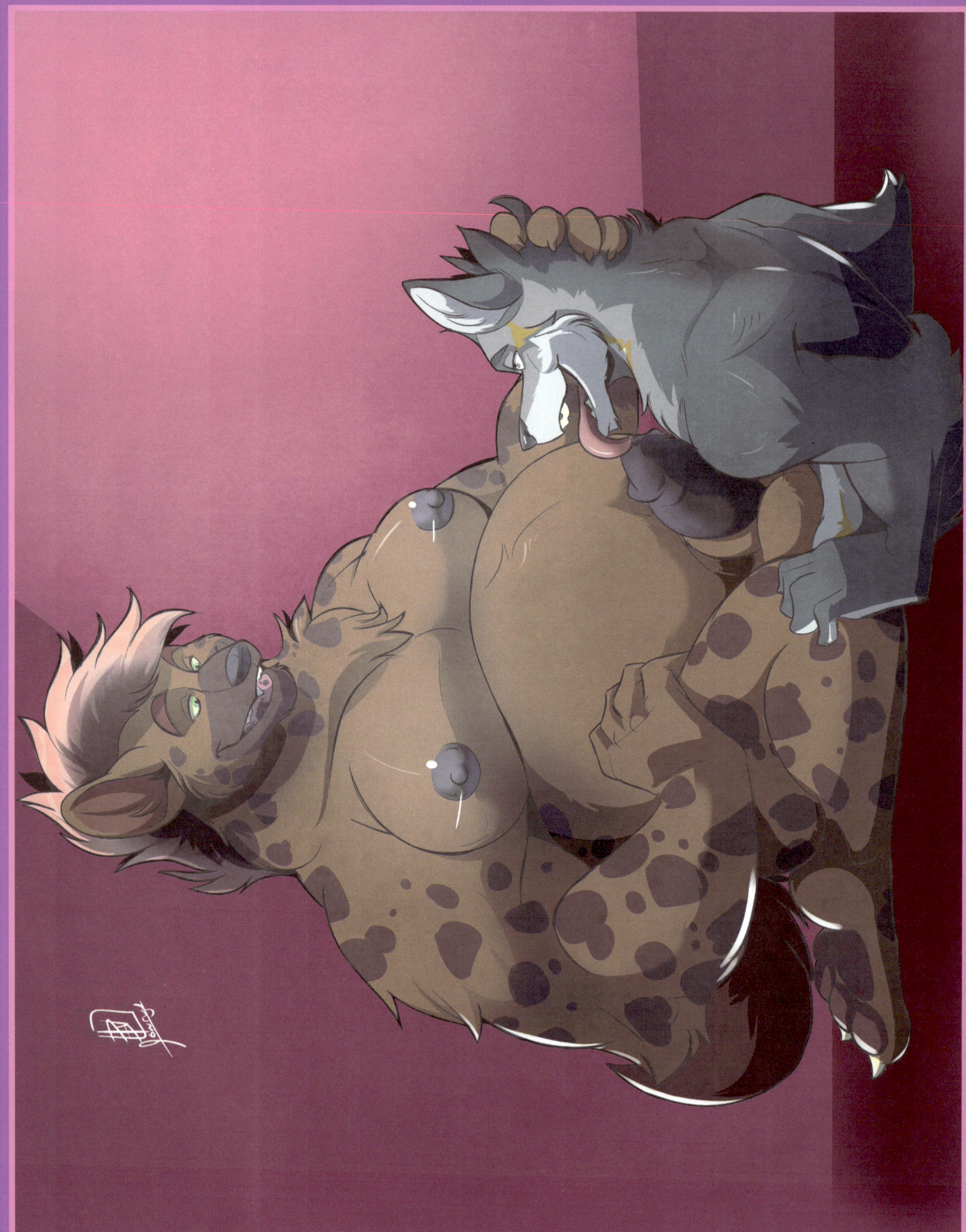

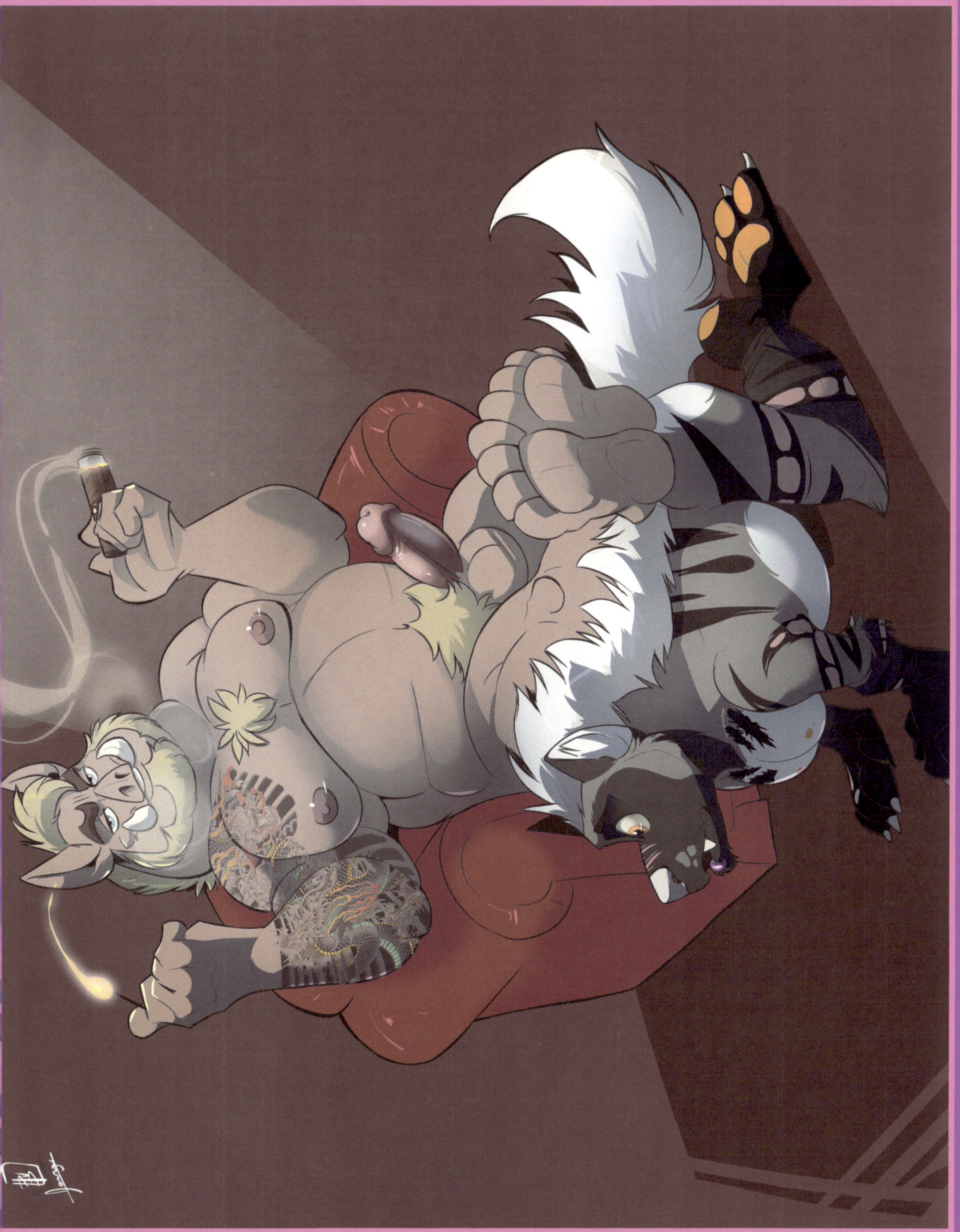

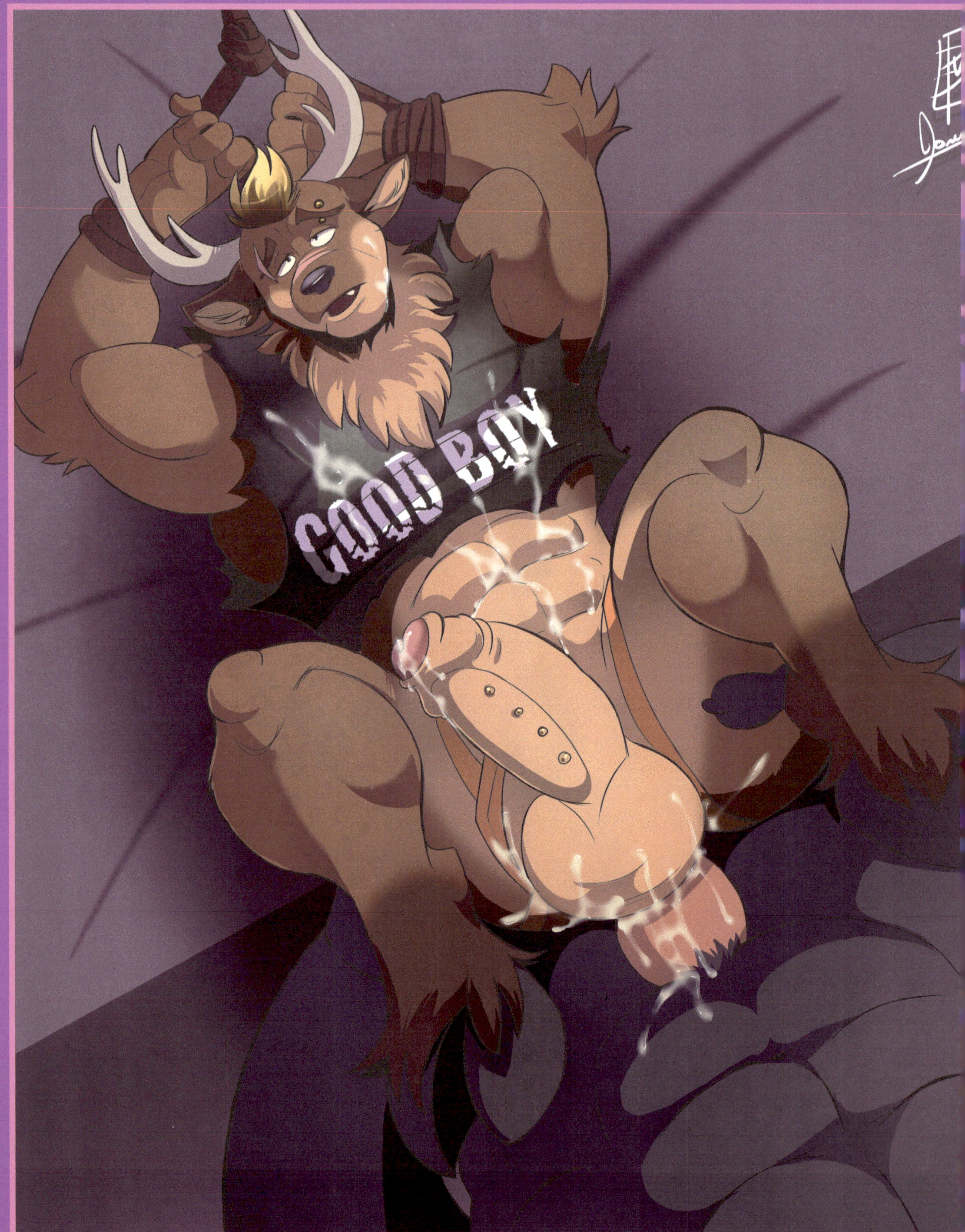
GOOD BOY

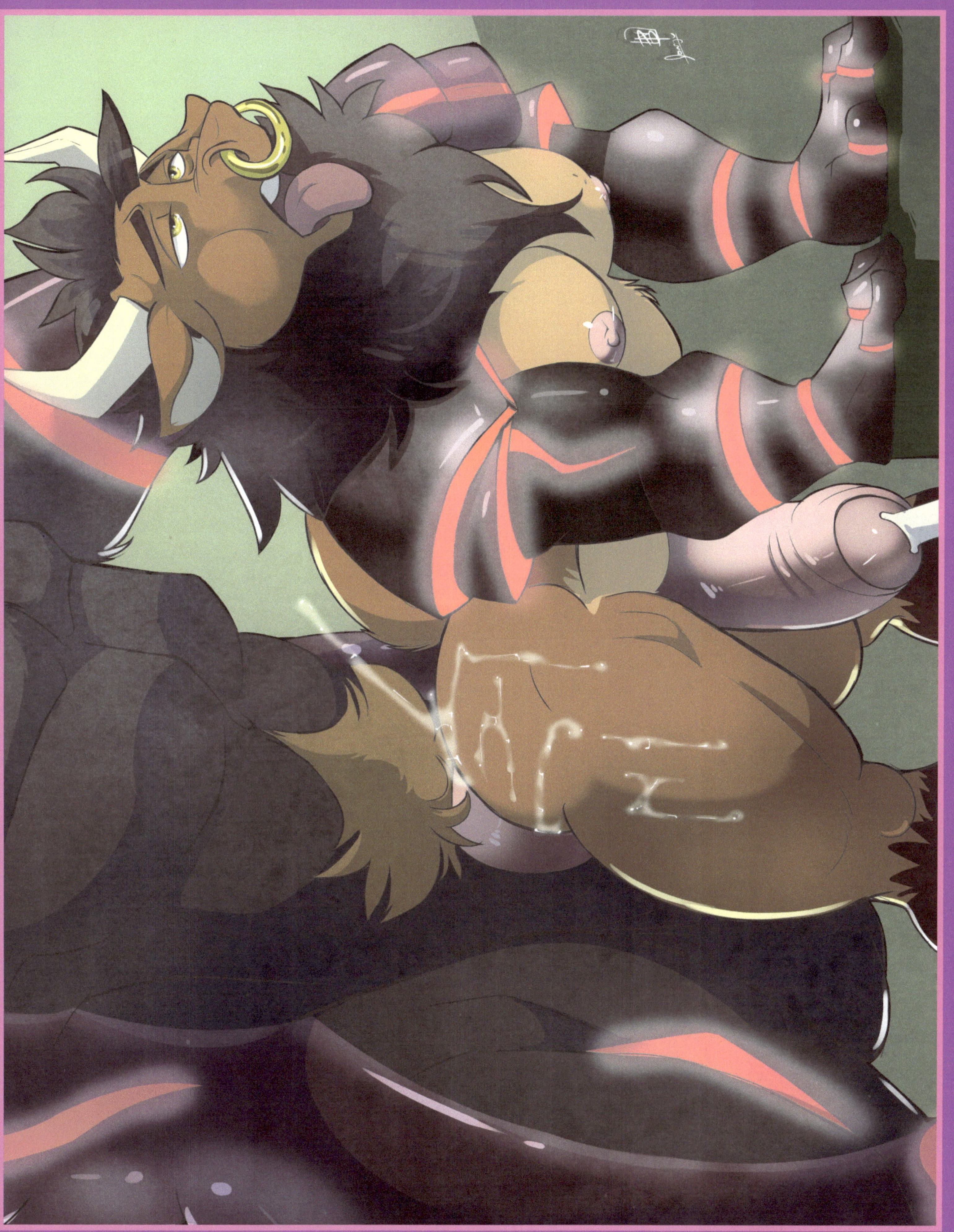

A Tail About a Fox

Our fandom is pretty familiar with the concept of folks discovering new aspects of themselves and becoming someone new. I think it's a beautiful feature of our fandom that we encourage people to grow and love themselves.

Leading into 2019 I lost someone very dear to me. My older brother- who was quite possibly the singular catalyst for my pursuit of art as a passion and career. I still carry a photo of myself sitting behind his art table at an anime con back in 2001.

Shortly after that we experienced a FREAKING PLAGUE. During and after that I continued to experience ordeal after ordeal. From scary medical emergencies to those close to me, to my own personal mental and emotional ordeals.

And I think I had to acknowledge that maybe I wasn't the same person going into 2019, that came out in 2021. And I think part of that reflection was becoming a Fox!

I've been able to explore a different side of myself with Vex the fox (Vex being the tiger AND the fox) and his various forms. Him being far more assertive, dominant in either form. Less apprehensive about putting himself out there and willing to challenge his company (but, in a kind way, never an antagonizing way... Okay maybe a little bit, just never mean spirited).

This is not the end of the tiger, but more of an addition to the cast. Much as there's many aspects of myself from before that I still feel are part of me, but now that I acknowledge that there is more to me, I want those features to have a voice too.

We all treat our own characters and what we associate with those species differently, but they are often personal and true to ourselves.

I've been told that the way I've characterized both my tiger and fox personas has been contradictory of how they are often used in the fandom. Well, I don't think I'd be the first person walking around as a floating mass of contradictions.

Thanks for letting me take a moment to spend time thinking on this particular topic. I often spend time just neck deep in work and doing my best. Taking a moment to self reflect has been somewhat cathartic.

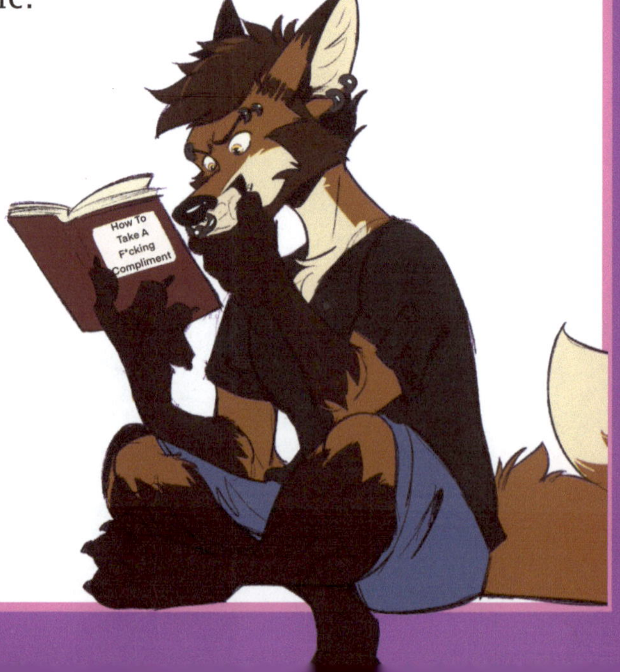

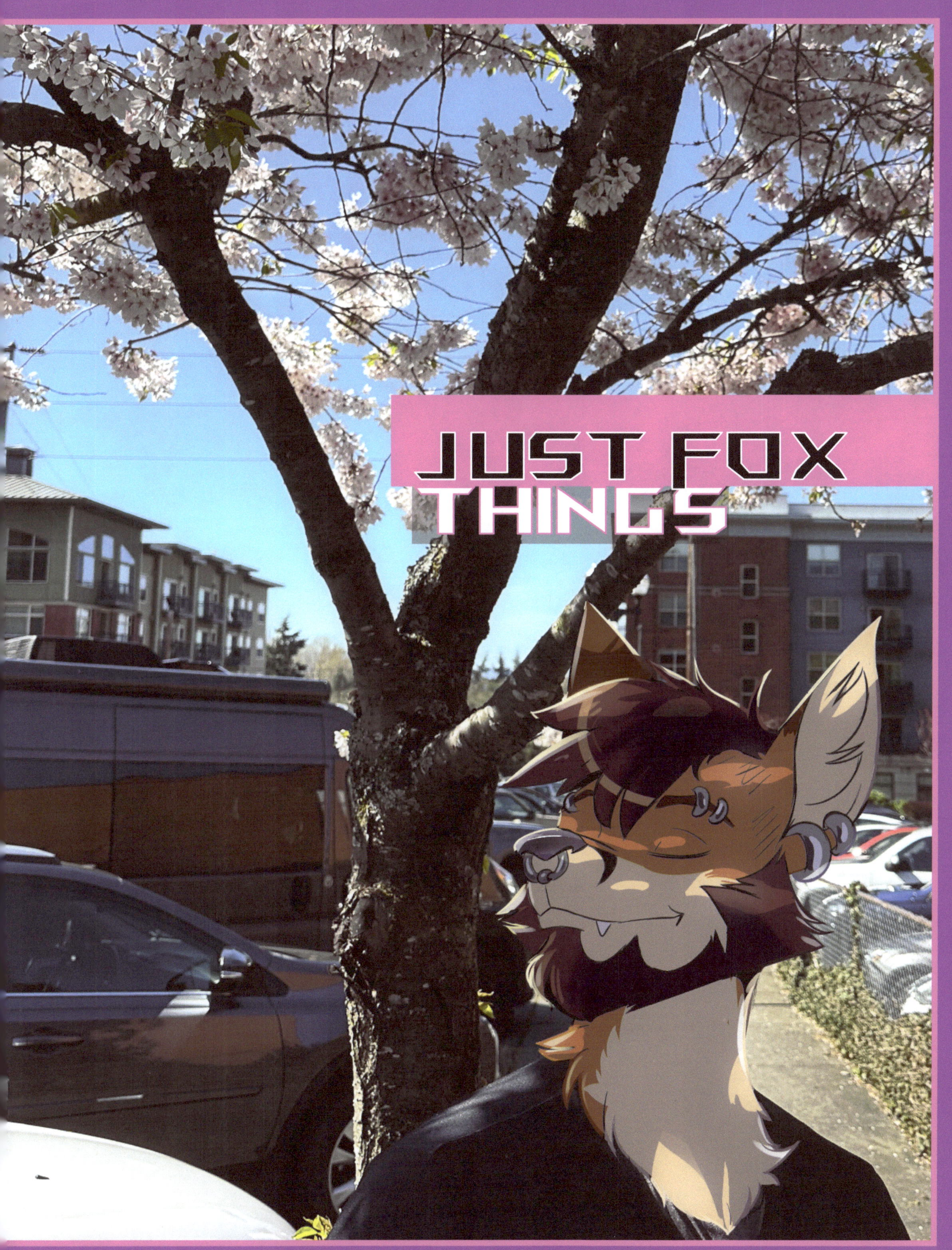
JUST FOX
THINGS

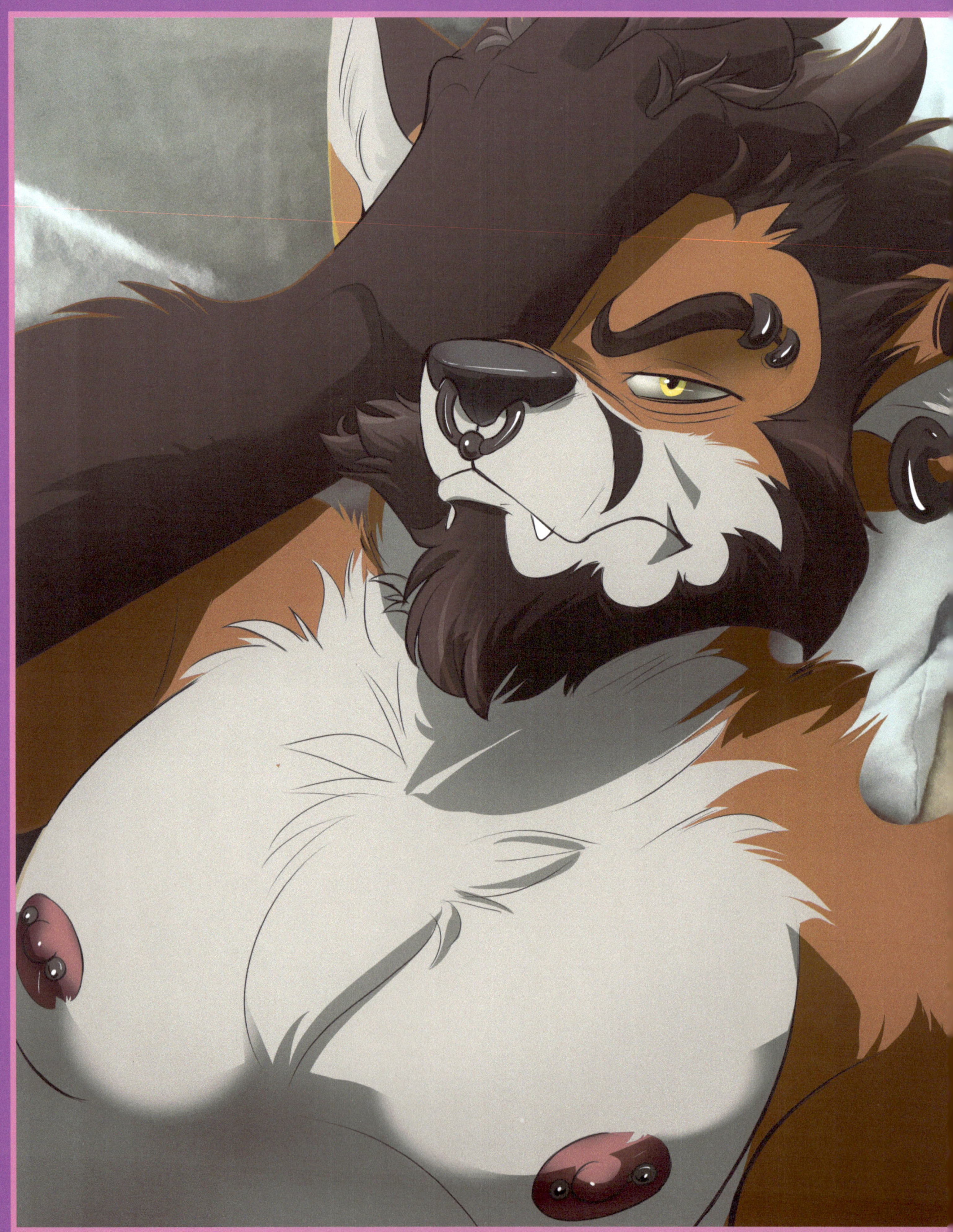

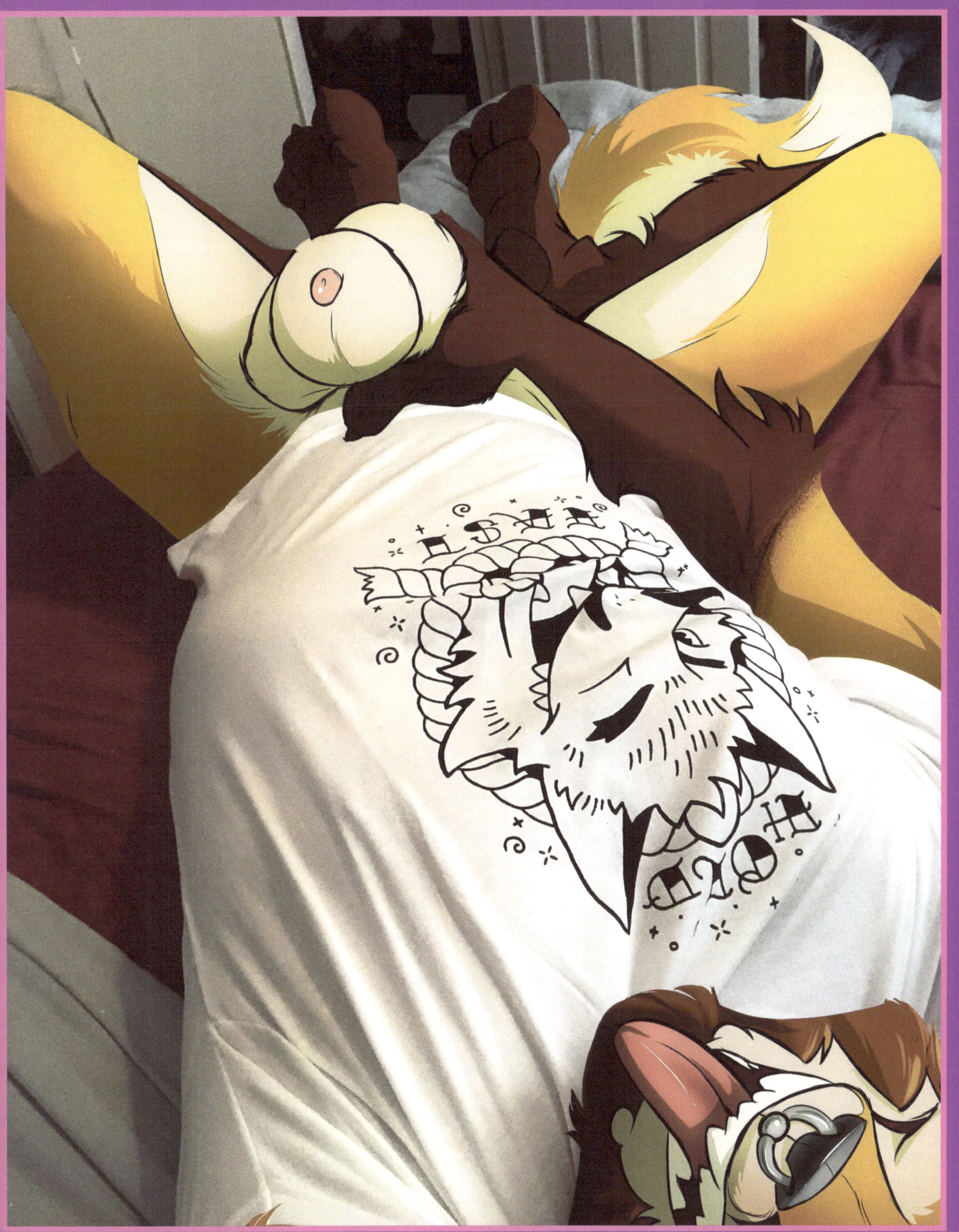
HOLD
FAST

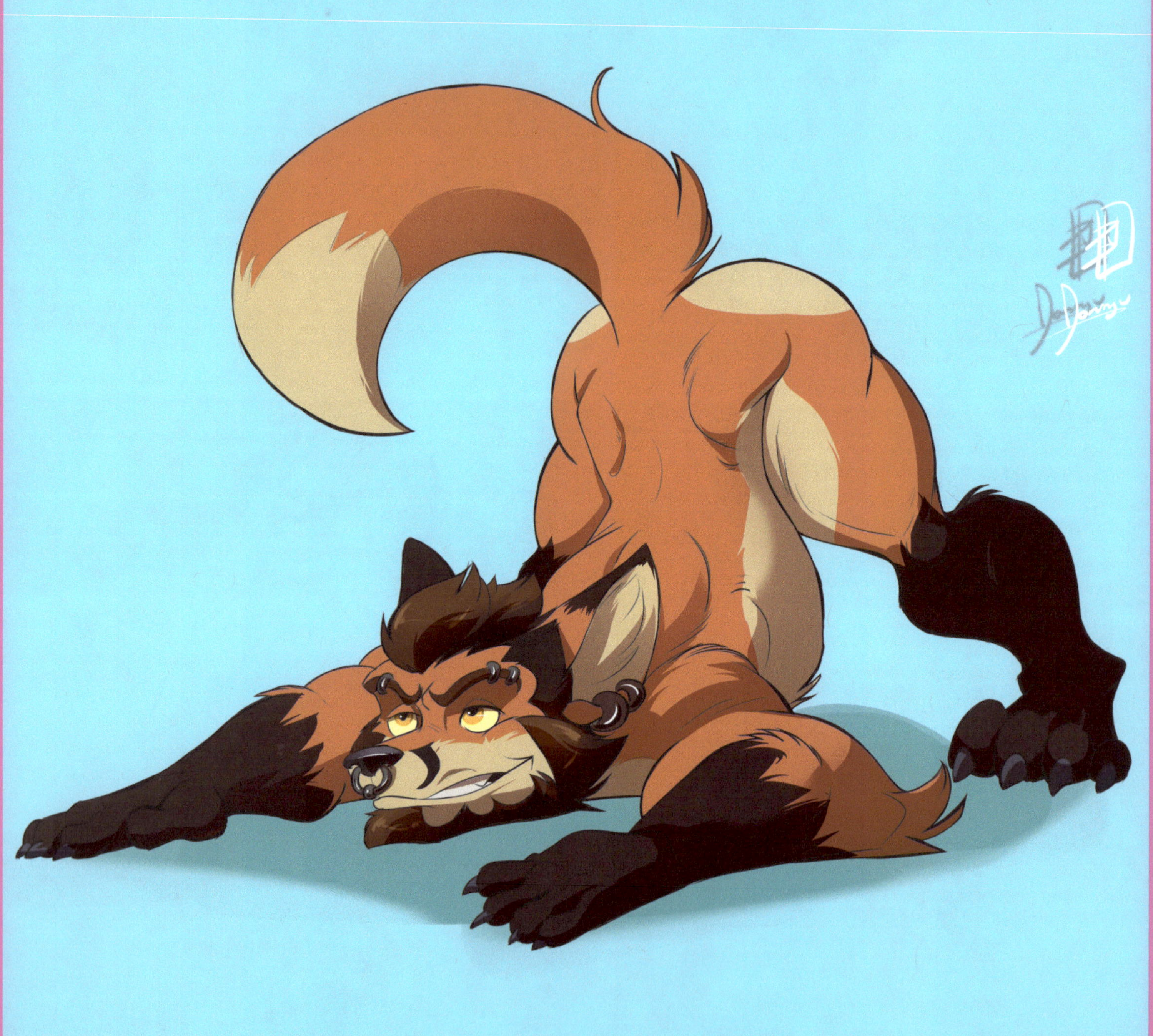

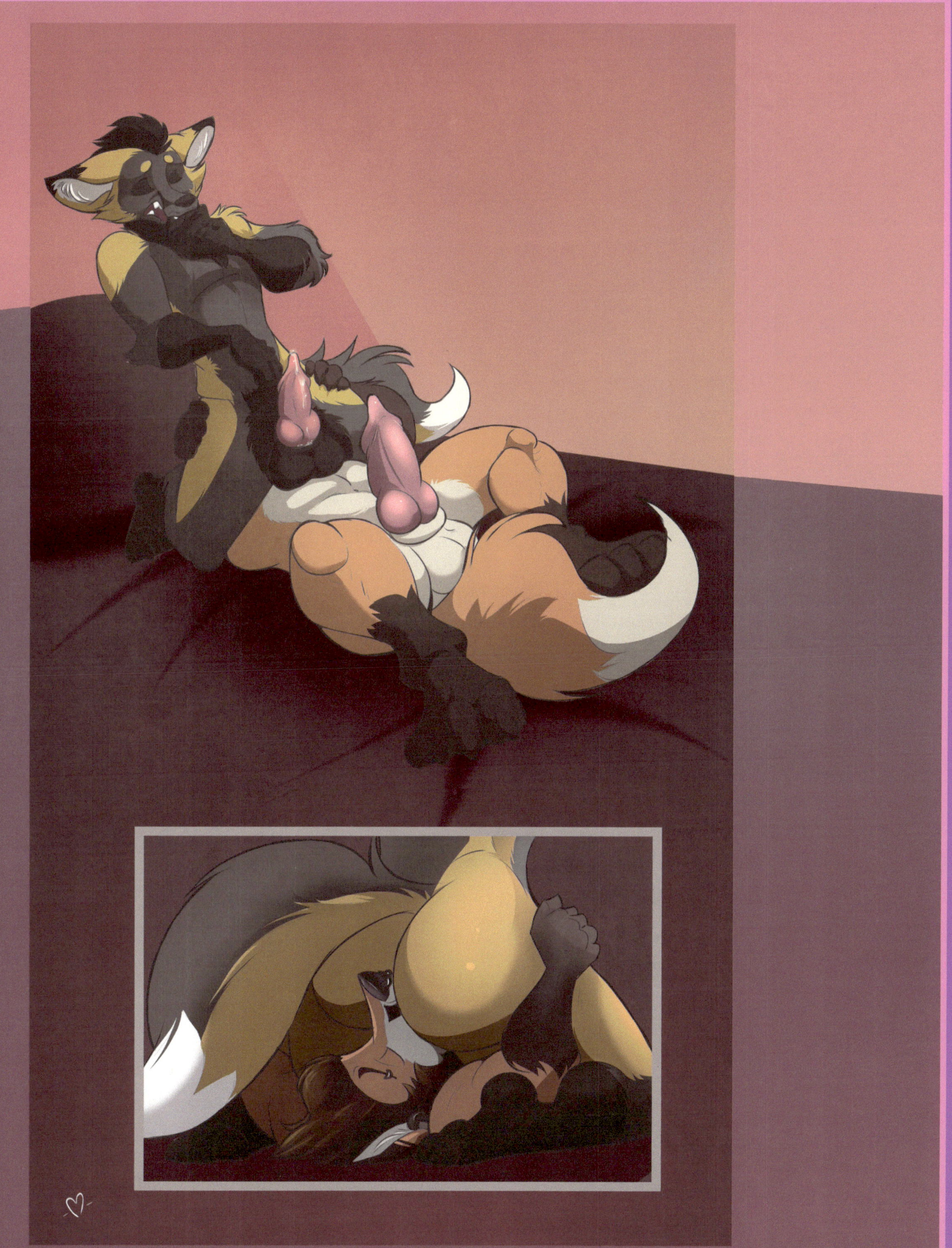

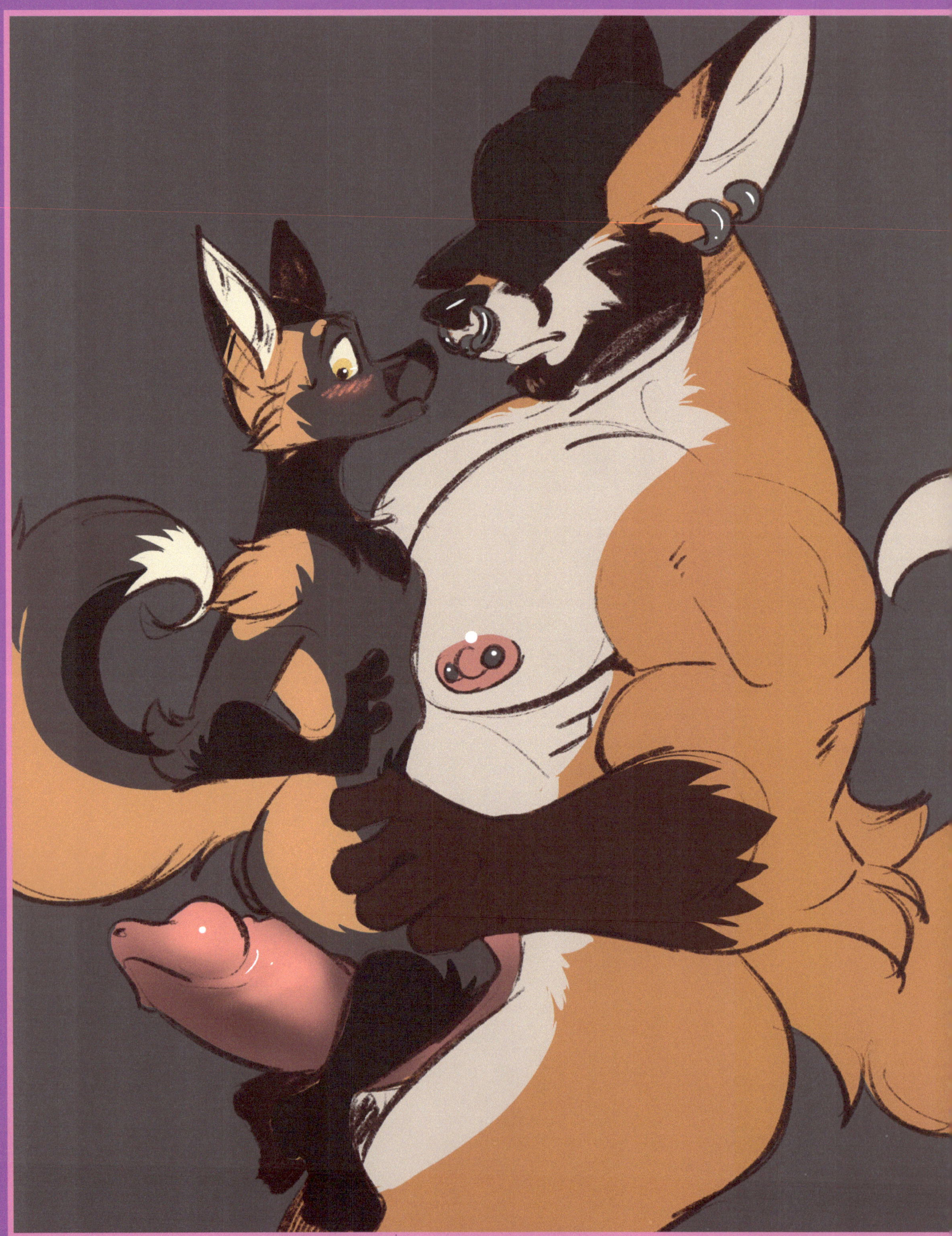

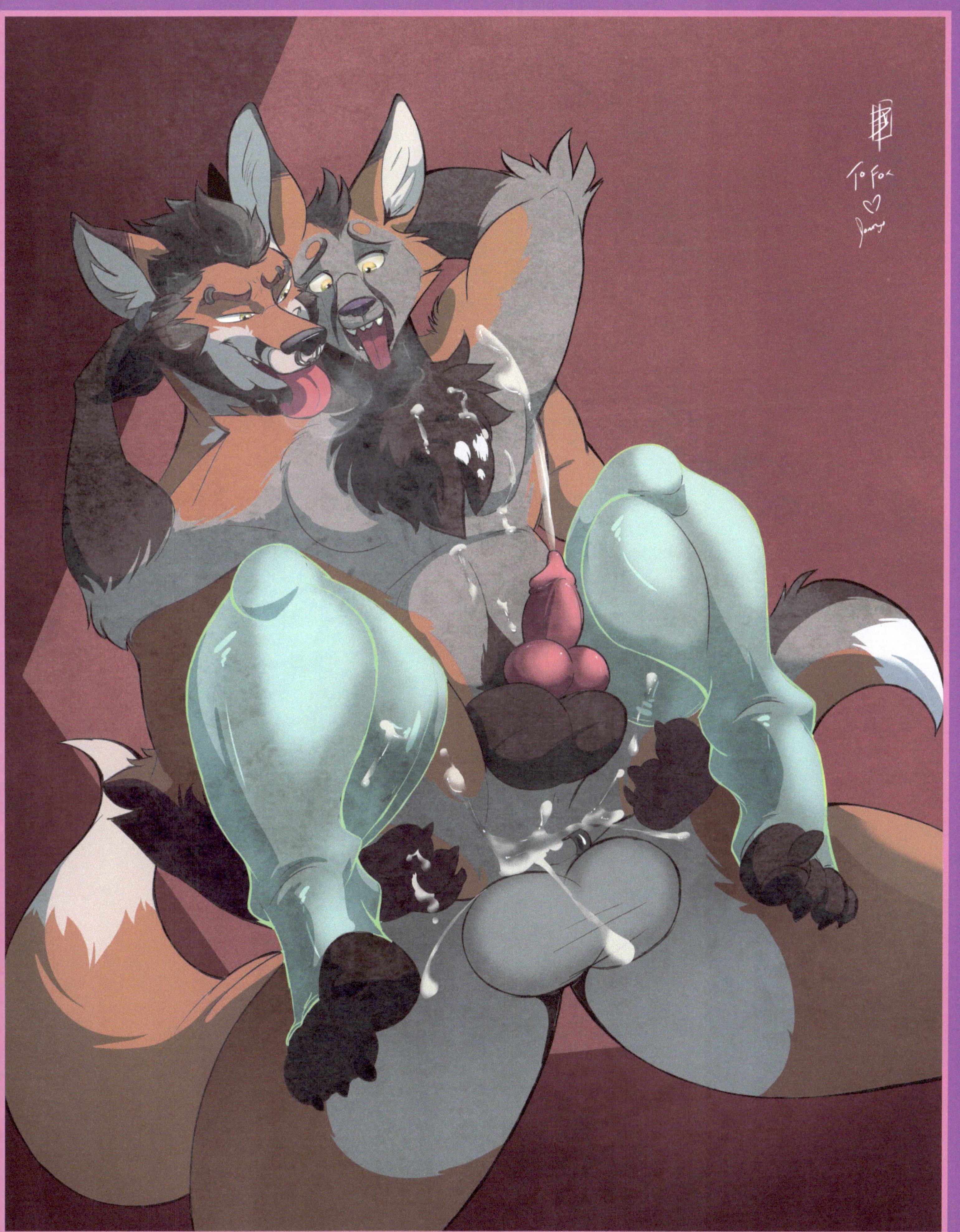
To Fox

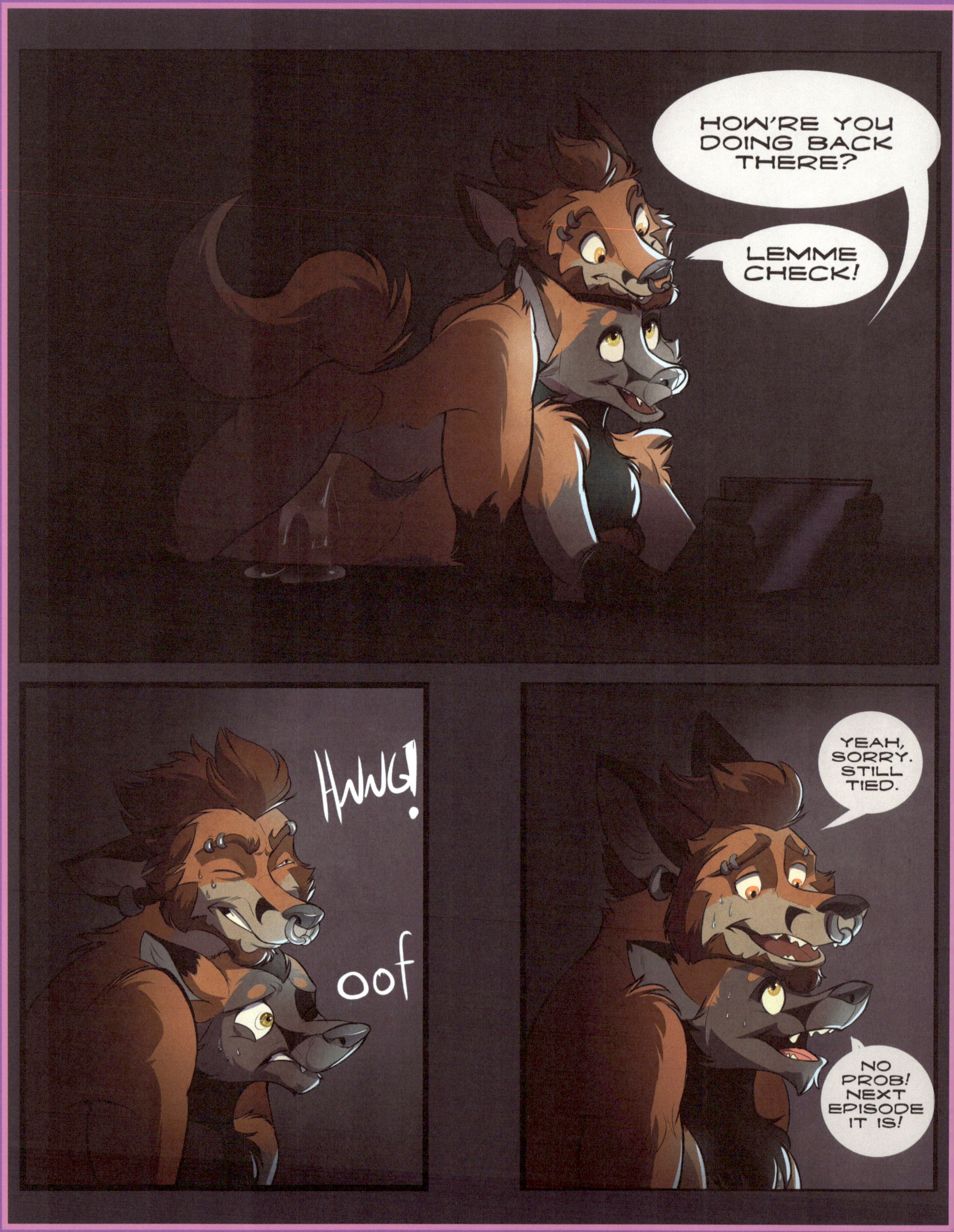

HOW'RE YOU DOING BACK THERE?
LEMME CHECK!

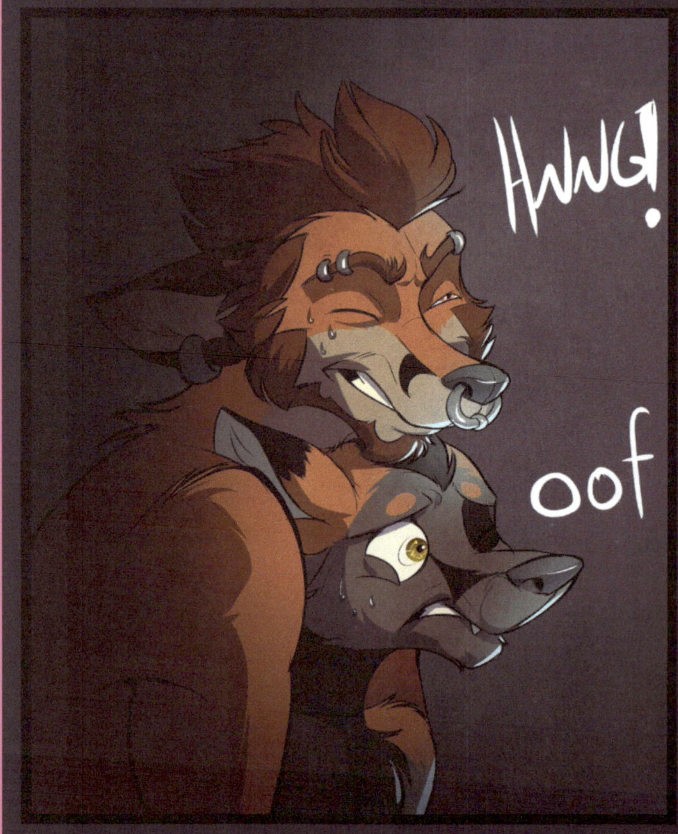

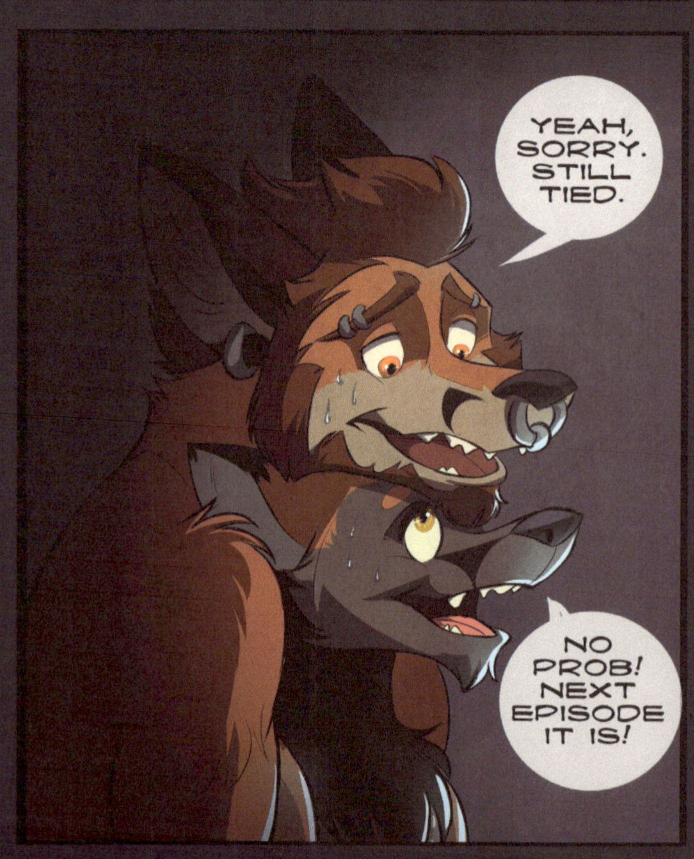

GONNA FINISH THE WHOLE SEASON AT THIS POINT.
"Lemme tell ya there Bob-o either this kid has a light bulb up his butt or his colon has a great idea."

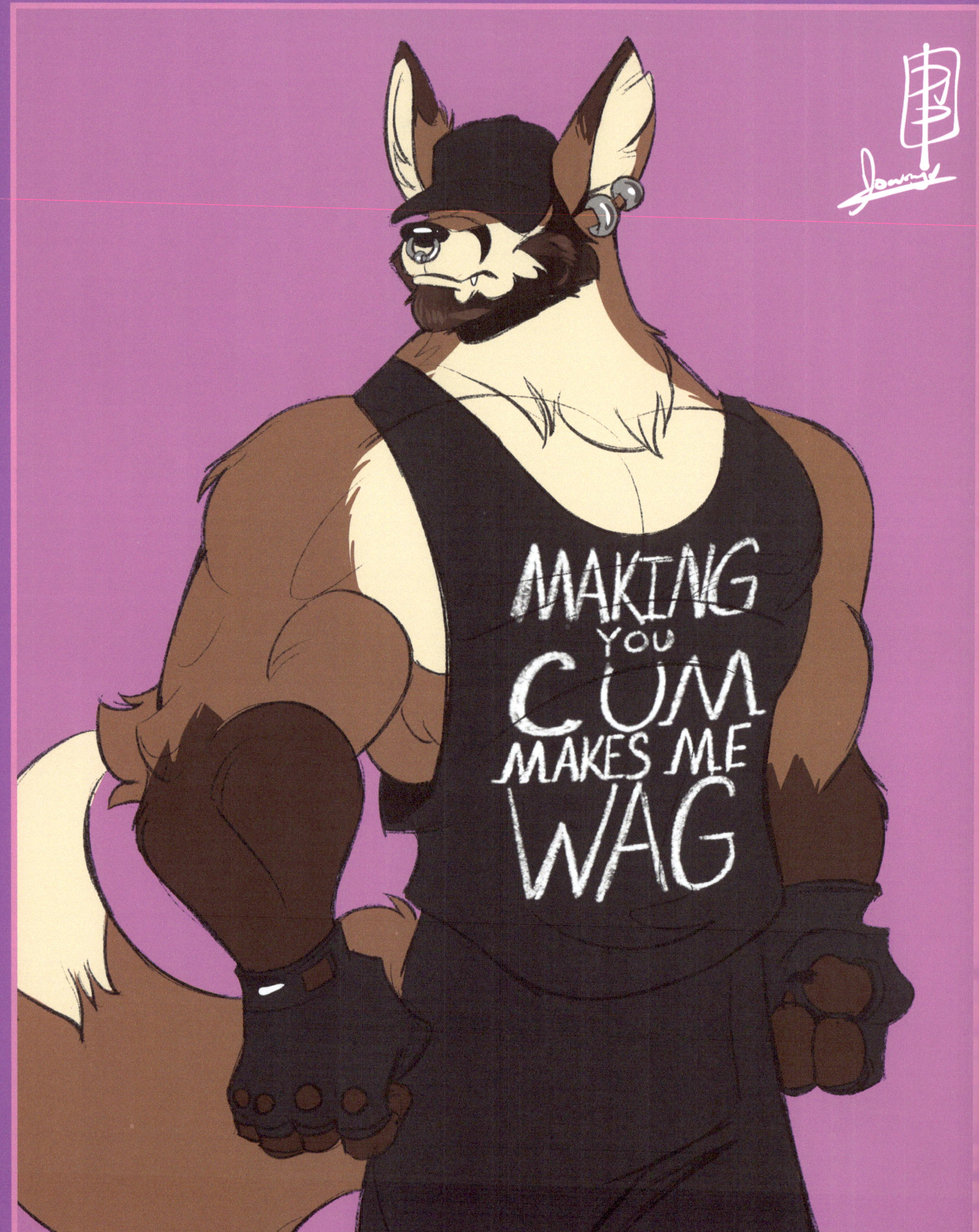
MAKING YOU CUM MAKES ME WAG

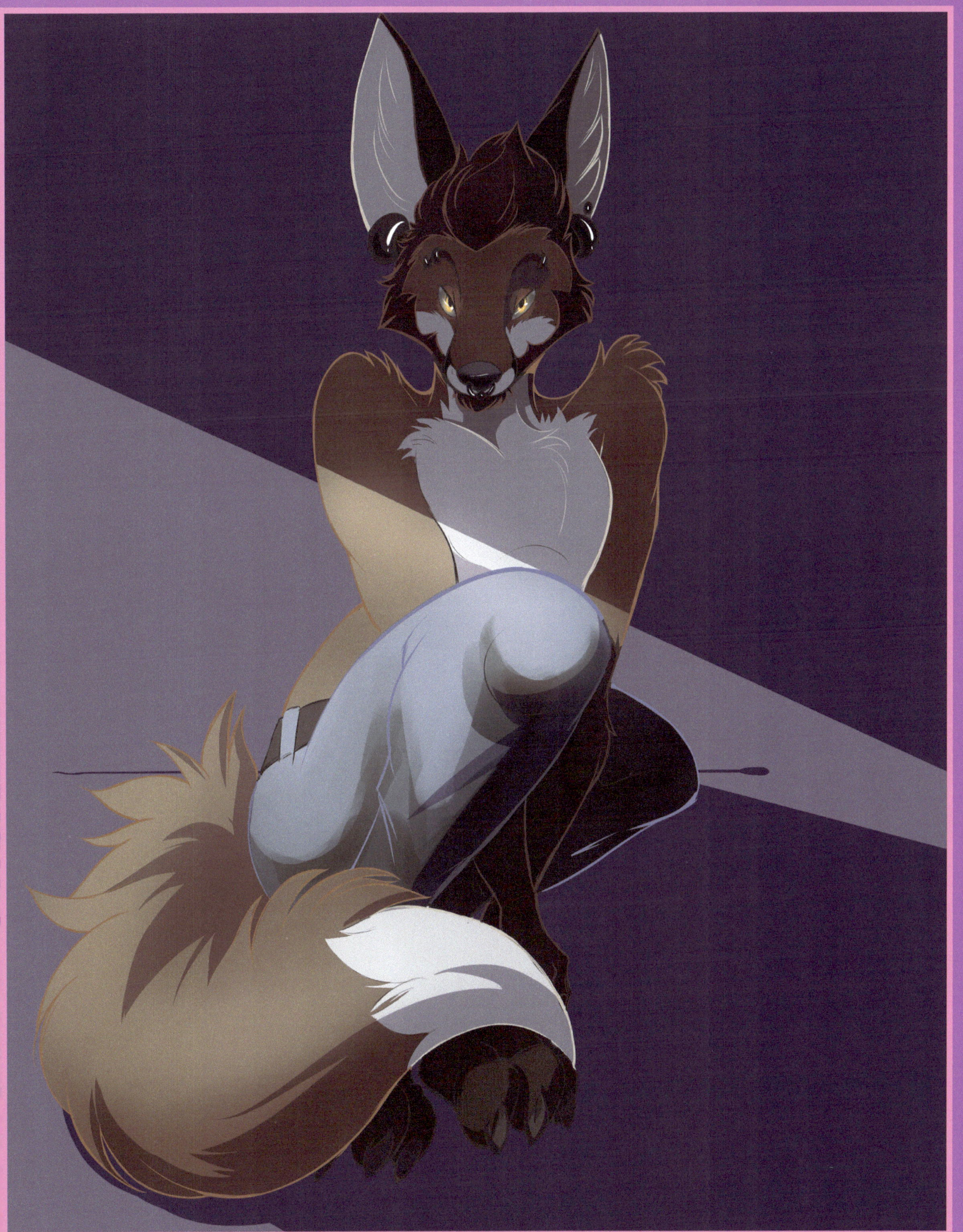

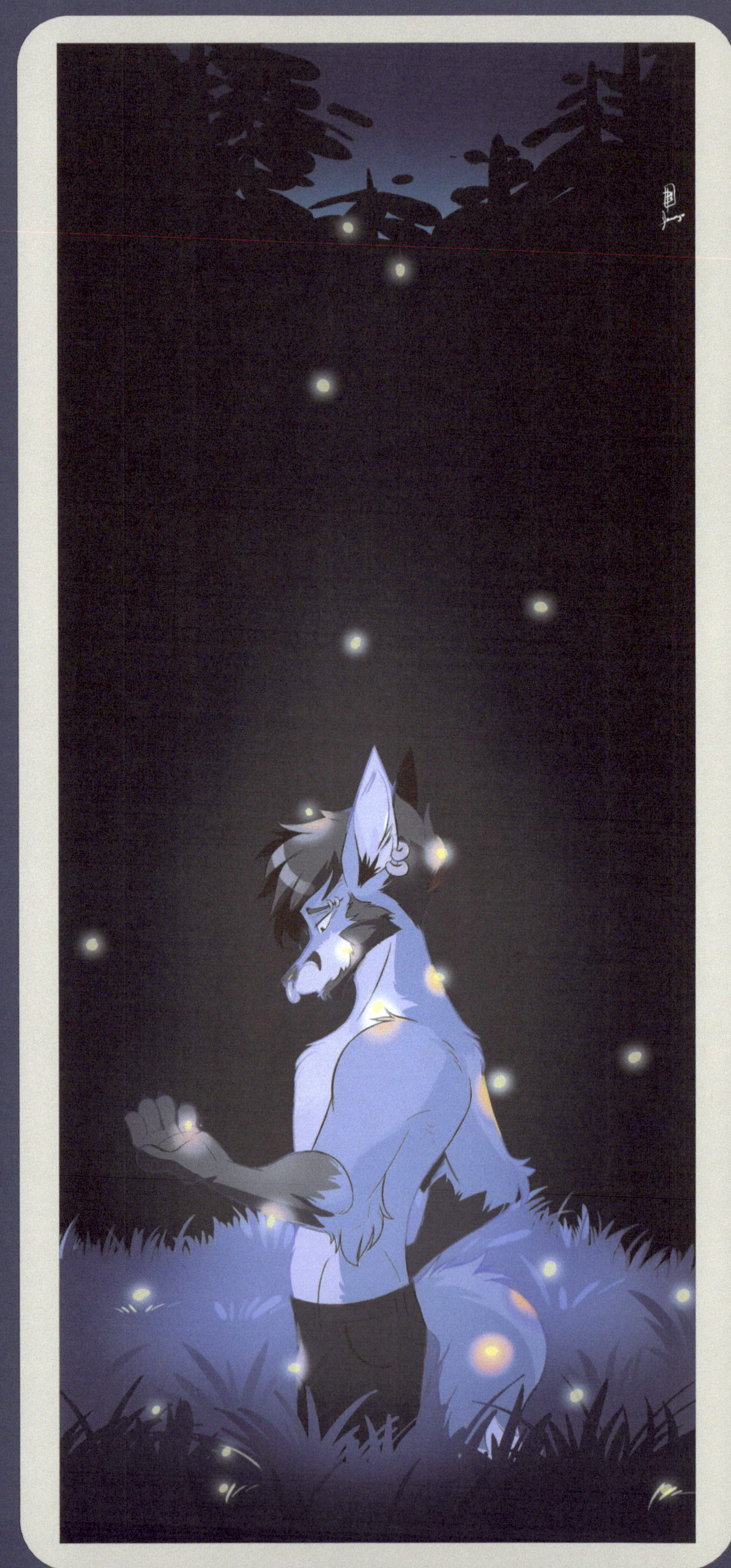

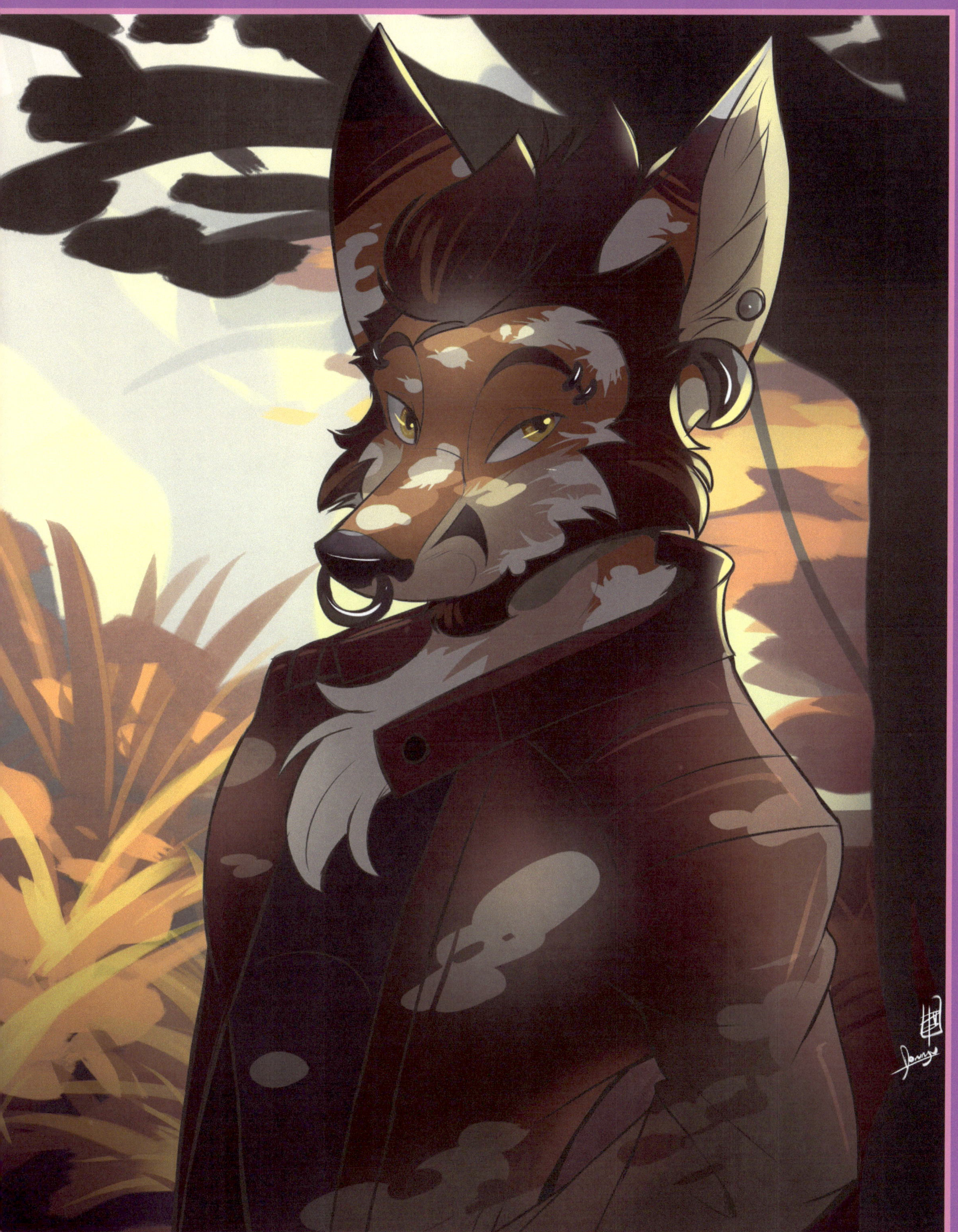

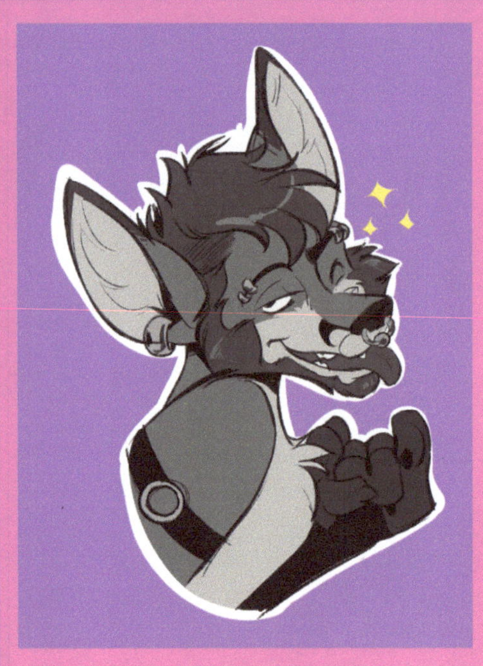

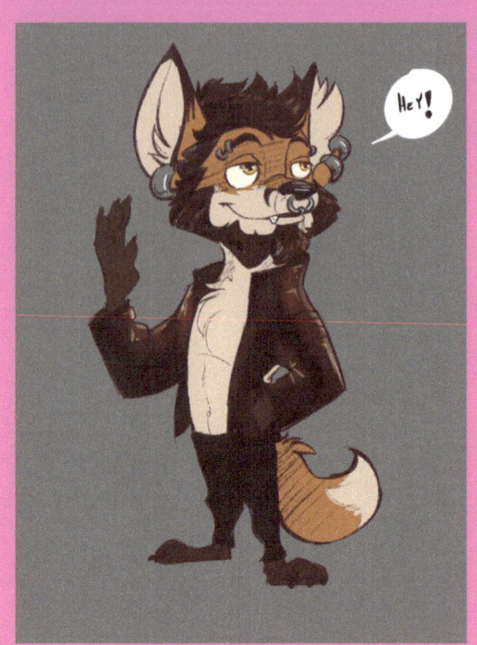
HEY!

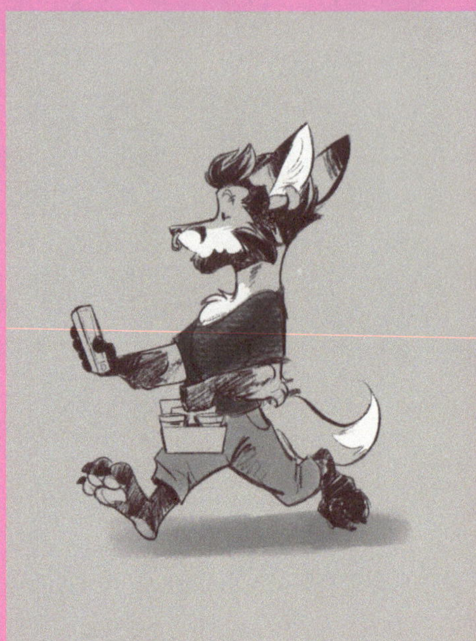

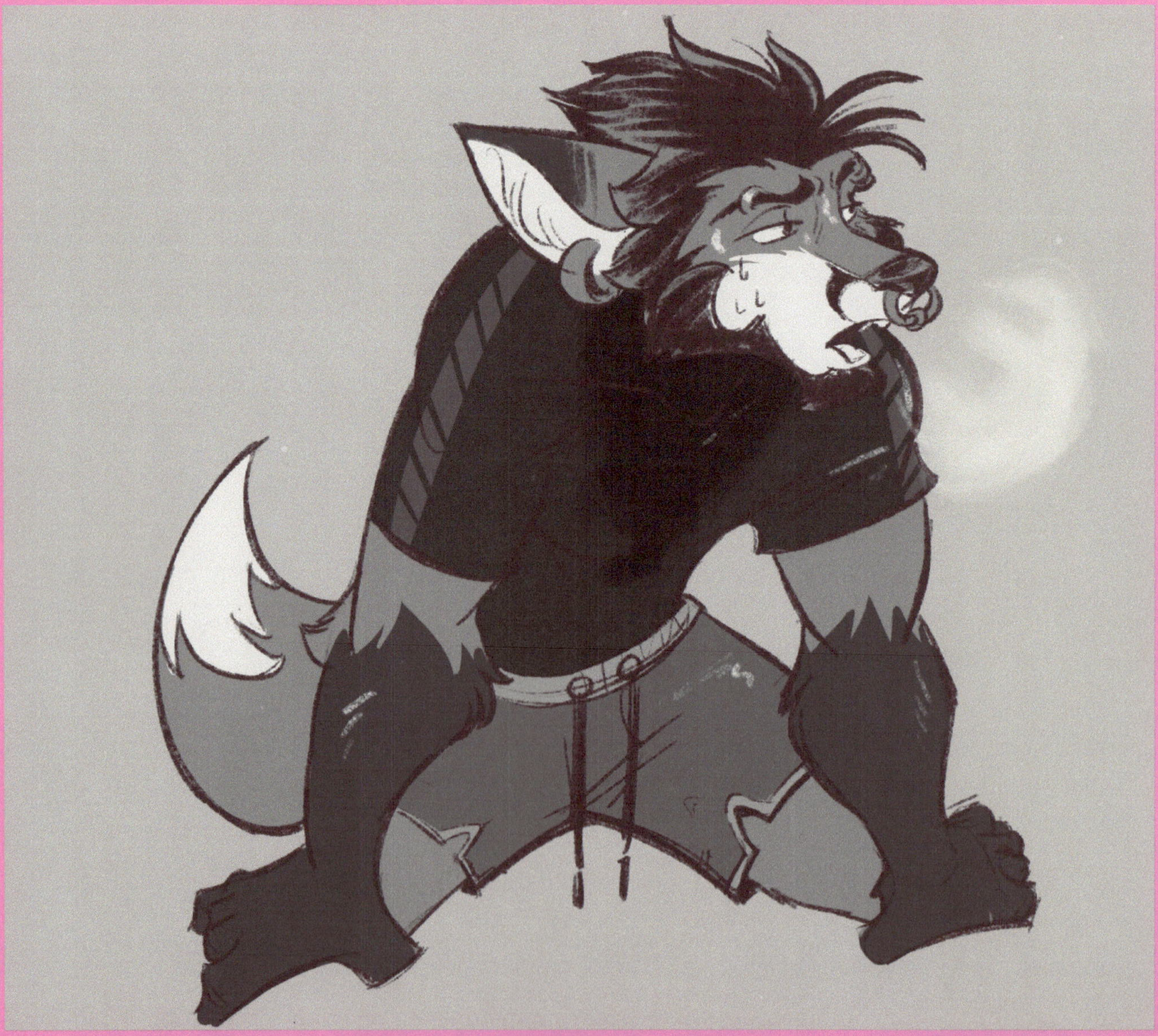

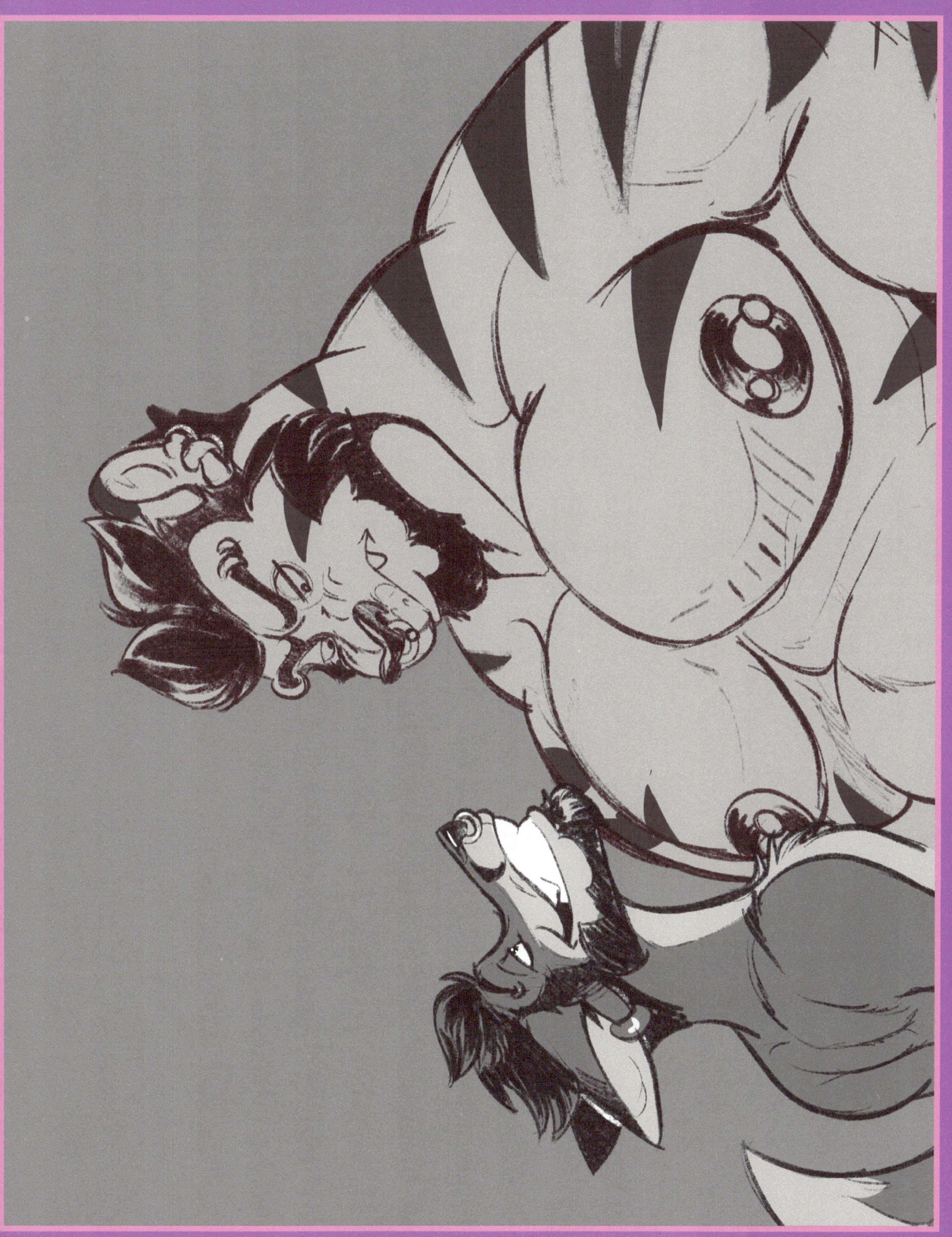

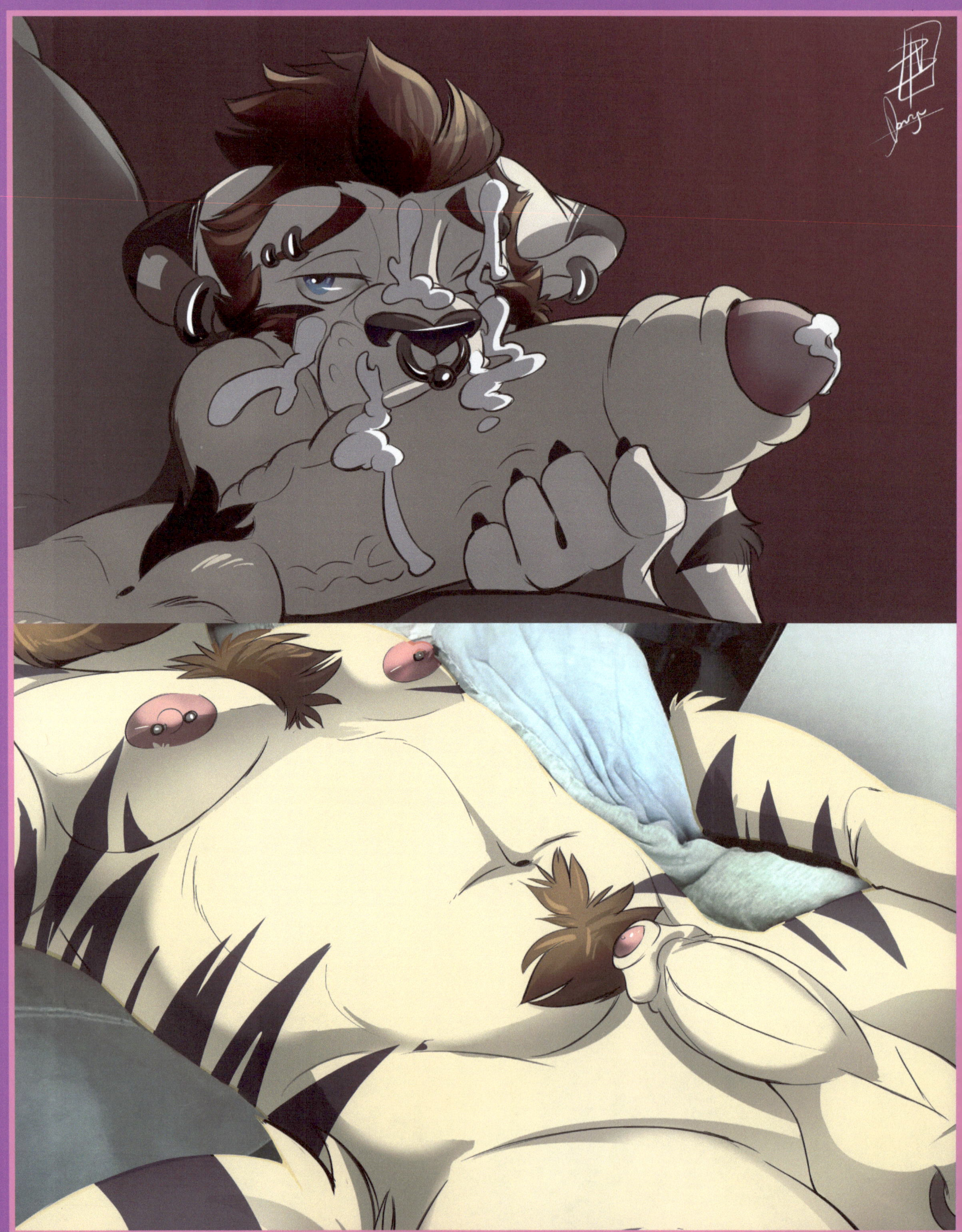

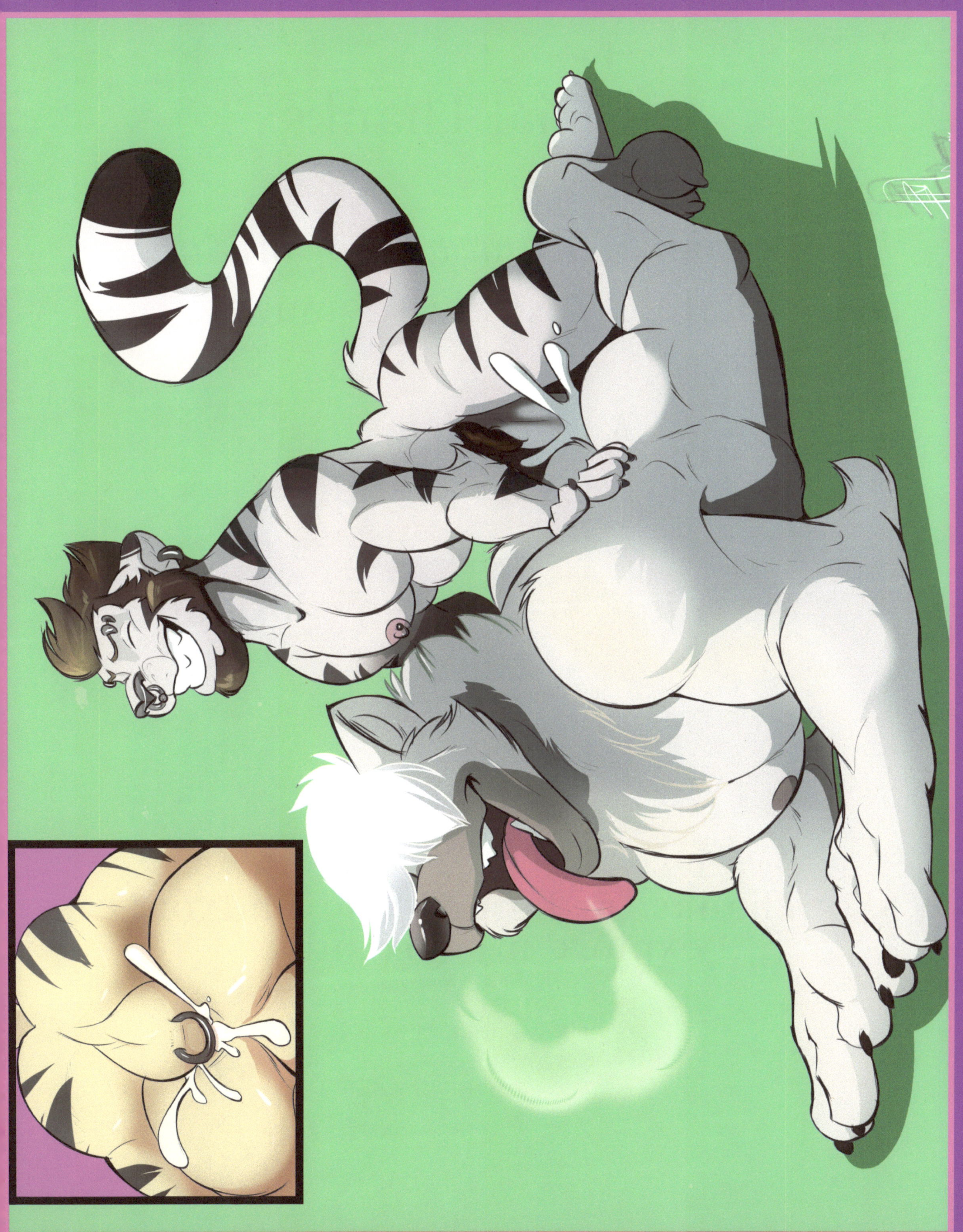

Special Thanks

My partner and love of my life:

Ralph "Zexyz" Greymuzzle

My best friends:

Erin, Amon, Tredain

My editor, friend and confidant:

Teiran

And to:

Tryk

Thanks for helping me find and explore my Fox side.

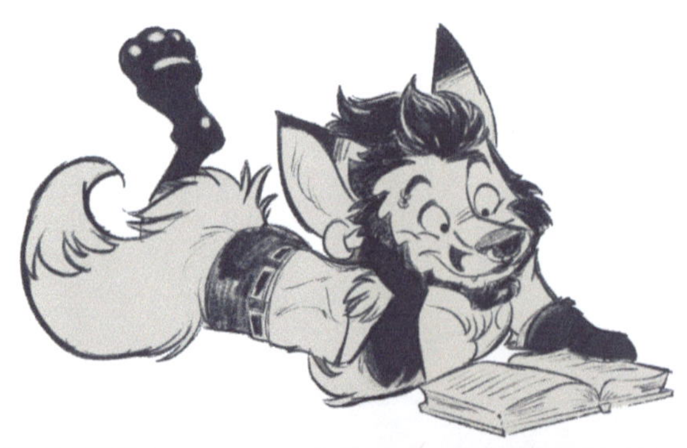

www.ingramcontent.com/pod-product-compliance
Lightning Source LLC
LaVergne TN
LVHW070507120826
845147LV00031BA/257